GRAPHIC LIBRARY™

INVENTIONS AND DISCOVERY

# ELI WHITNEY AND THE COTTON GIN

by Jessica Gunderson

illustrated by Gerry Acerno, Rodney Ramos,
and Charles Barnett III

**Consultant:**
Regan Huff
Special Projects Consultant
Eli Whitney Museum

Capstone
press®

Mankato, Minnesota

Graphic Library is published by Capstone Press,
151 Good Counsel Drive, P.O. Box 669, Mankato, Minnesota 56002.
www.capstonepress.com


Printed in the United States of America

1 2 3 4 5 6 12 11 10 09 08 07

*Library of Congress Cataloging-in-Publication Data*
Gunderson, Jessica.
Eli Whitney and the cotton gin / by Jessica Gunderson; illustrated by Gerry Acerno, Rodney Ramos, and Charles Barnett III.
p. cm.—(Graphic library. Inventions and discovery)
Summary: "In graphic novel format, tells the story of how Eli Whitney invented the cotton gin, and the effects it had on the South"—Provided by publisher.
Includes bibliographical references and index.
ISBN–13: 978-0-7368-6843-3 (hardcover)
ISBN–10: 0-7368-6843-7 (hardcover)
ISBN–13: 978-0-7368-7895-1 (softcover pbk.)
ISBN–10: 0-7368-7895-5 (softcover pbk.)
1. Whitney, Eli, 1765–1825—Juvenile literature. 2. Inventors—United States—Biography—Juvenile literature. 3. Cotton gins and ginning—Juvenile literature. I. Acerno, Gerry, ill. II. Ramos, Rodney, ill. III. Barnett, Charles, III ill. IV. Title. V. Series.
TS1570.W4G86 2007
677'.2121092—dc22 2006026399

*Designer*
Jason Knudson

*Colorist*
Cynthia Martin

*Editor*
Aaron Sautter

**Editor's note:** Direct quotations from primary sources are indicated by a yellow background.

Direct quotations appear on the following pages:
Page 9 from *Memoir of Eli Whitney, Esq.* by Denison Olmsted (New York: Arno Press, 1972).
Pages 19 and 22 from *The World of Eli Whitney* by Jeanette Mirsky and Allan Nevins (New York: Macmillan, 1952).
Page 23 from *Eli Whitney and the Birth of American Technology* by Constance McLaughlin Green (Boston: Little, Brown, 1956).

# TABLE OF CONTENTS

# Chapter 1
# The Seeds of an Idea

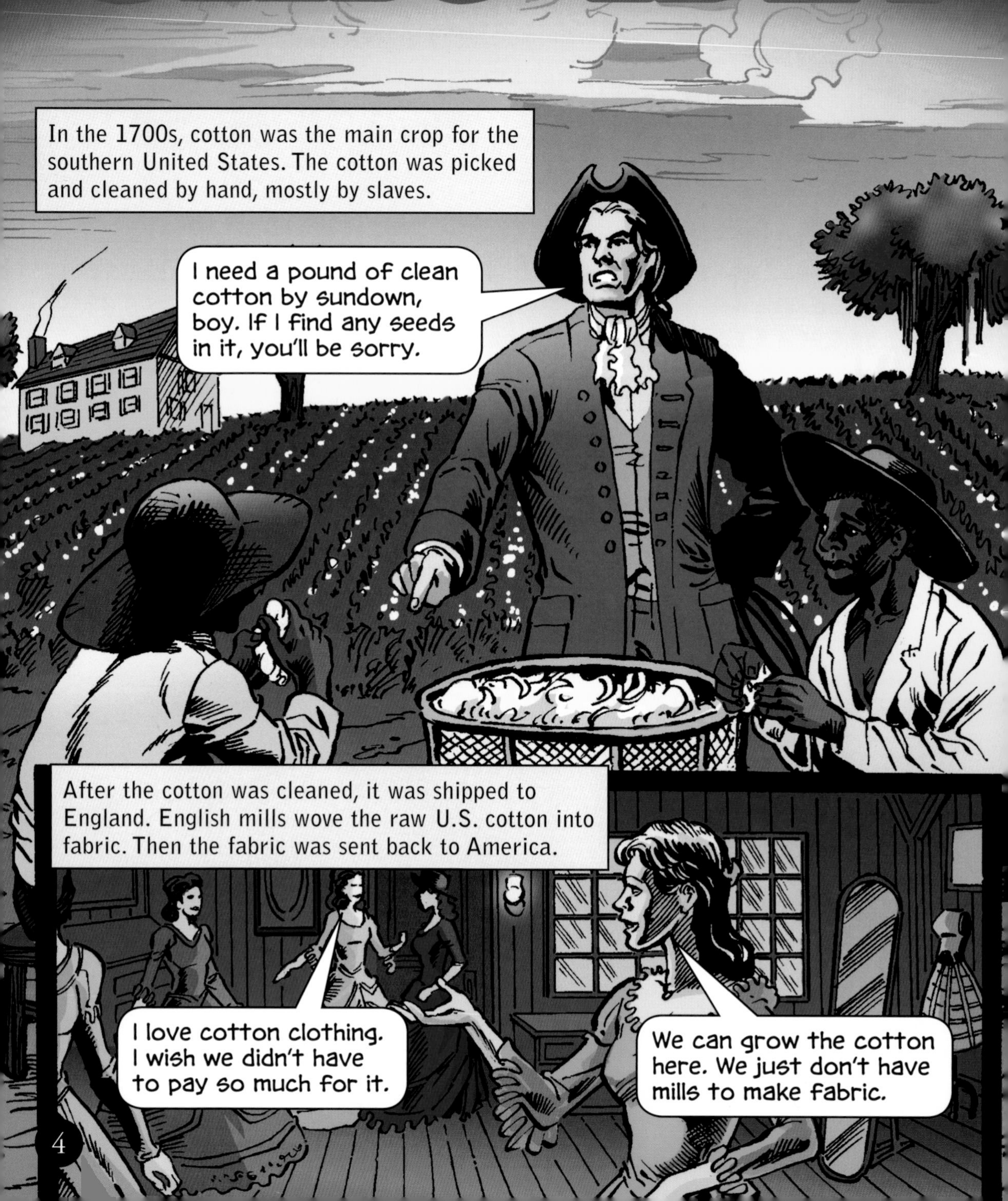
In the 1700s, cotton was the main crop for the southern United States. The cotton was picked and cleaned by hand, mostly by slaves.
I need a pound of clean cotton by sundown, boy. If I find any seeds in it, you'll be sorry.
After the cotton was cleaned, it was shipped to England. English mills wove the raw U.S. cotton into fabric. Then the fabric was sent back to America.
I love cotton clothing. I wish we didn't have to pay so much for it.
We can grow the cotton here. We just don't have mills to make fabric.

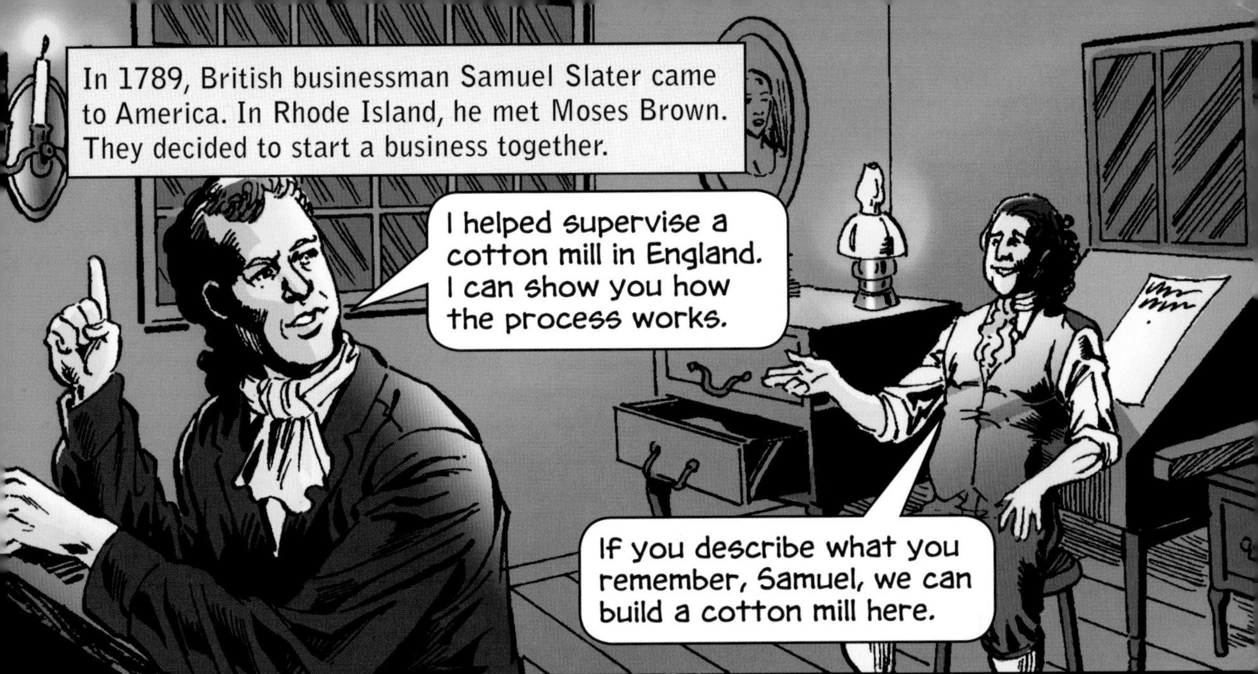
In 1789, British businessman Samuel Slater came to America. In Rhode Island, he met Moses Brown. They decided to start a business together.
I helped supervise a cotton mill in England. I can show you how the process works.
If you describe what you remember, Samuel, we can build a cotton mill here.

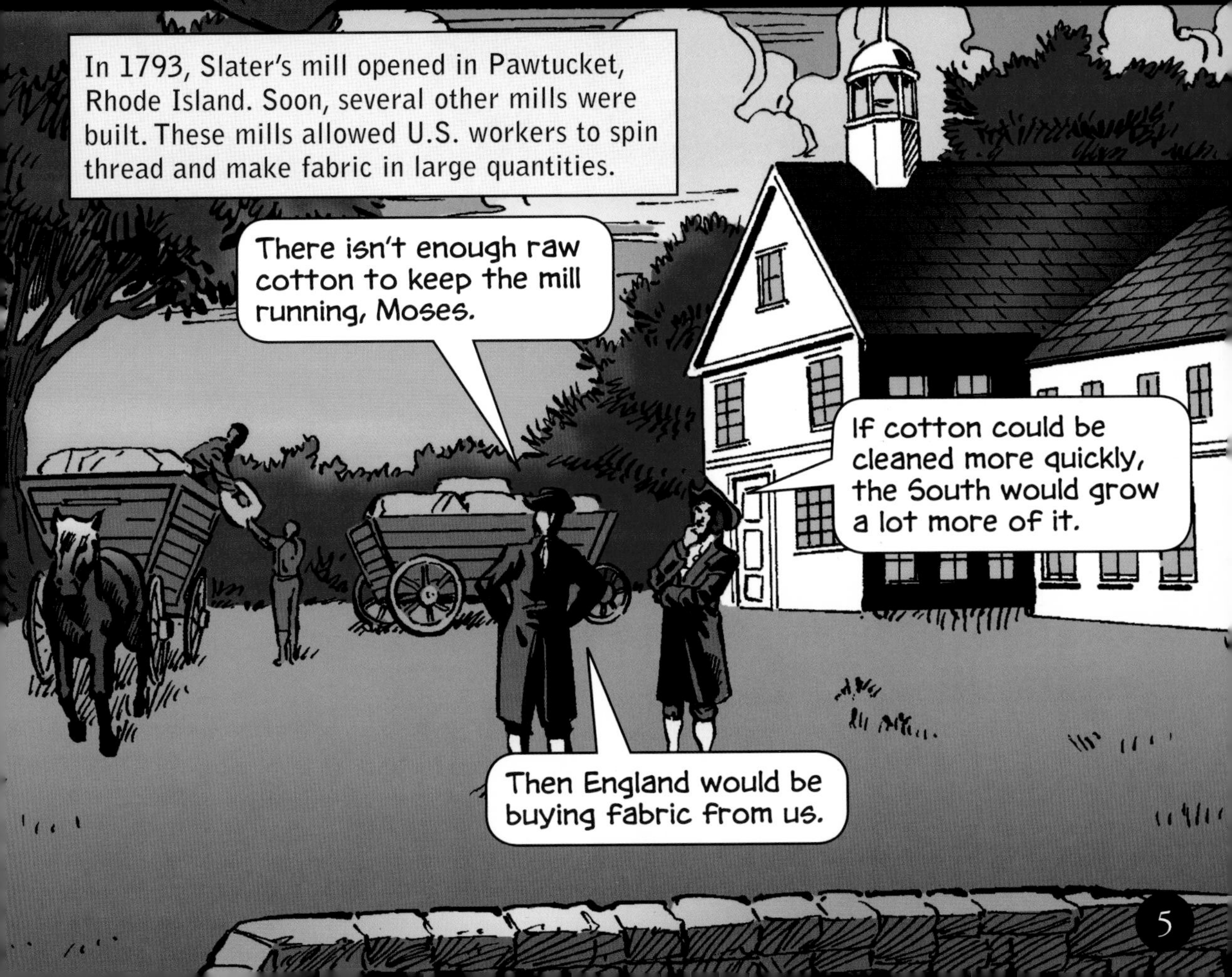
In 1793, Slater's mill opened in Pawtucket, Rhode Island. Soon, several other mills were built. These mills allowed U.S. workers to spin thread and make fabric in large quantities.
There isn't enough raw cotton to keep the mill running, Moses.
If cotton could be cleaned more quickly, the South would grow a lot more of it.
Then England would be buying fabric from us.

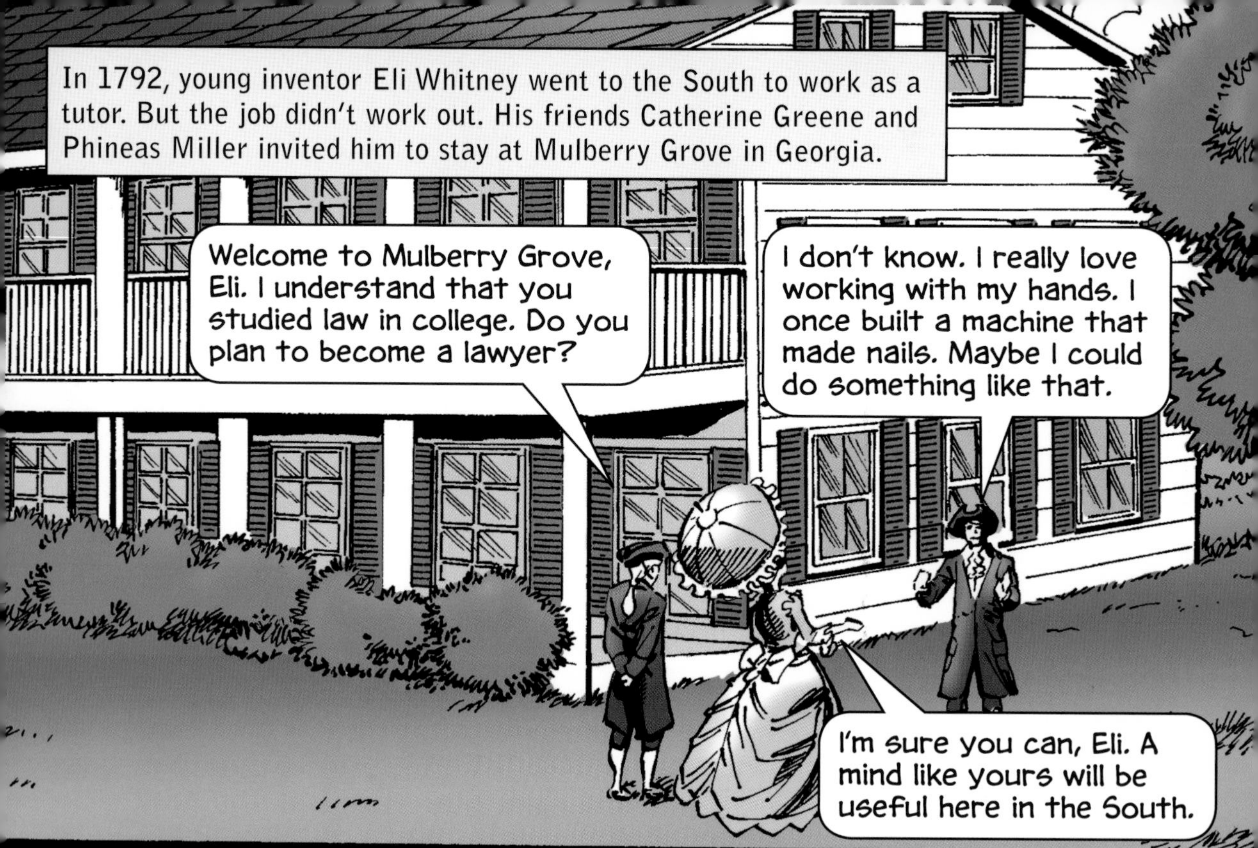
In 1792, young inventor Eli Whitney went to the South to work as a tutor. But the job didn't work out. His friends Catherine Greene and Phineas Miller invited him to stay at Mulberry Grove in Georgia.
Welcome to Mulberry Grove, Eli. I understand that you studied law in college. Do you plan to become a lawyer?
I don't know. I really love working with my hands. I once built a machine that made nails. Maybe I could do something like that.
I'm sure you can, Eli. A mind like yours will be useful here in the South.

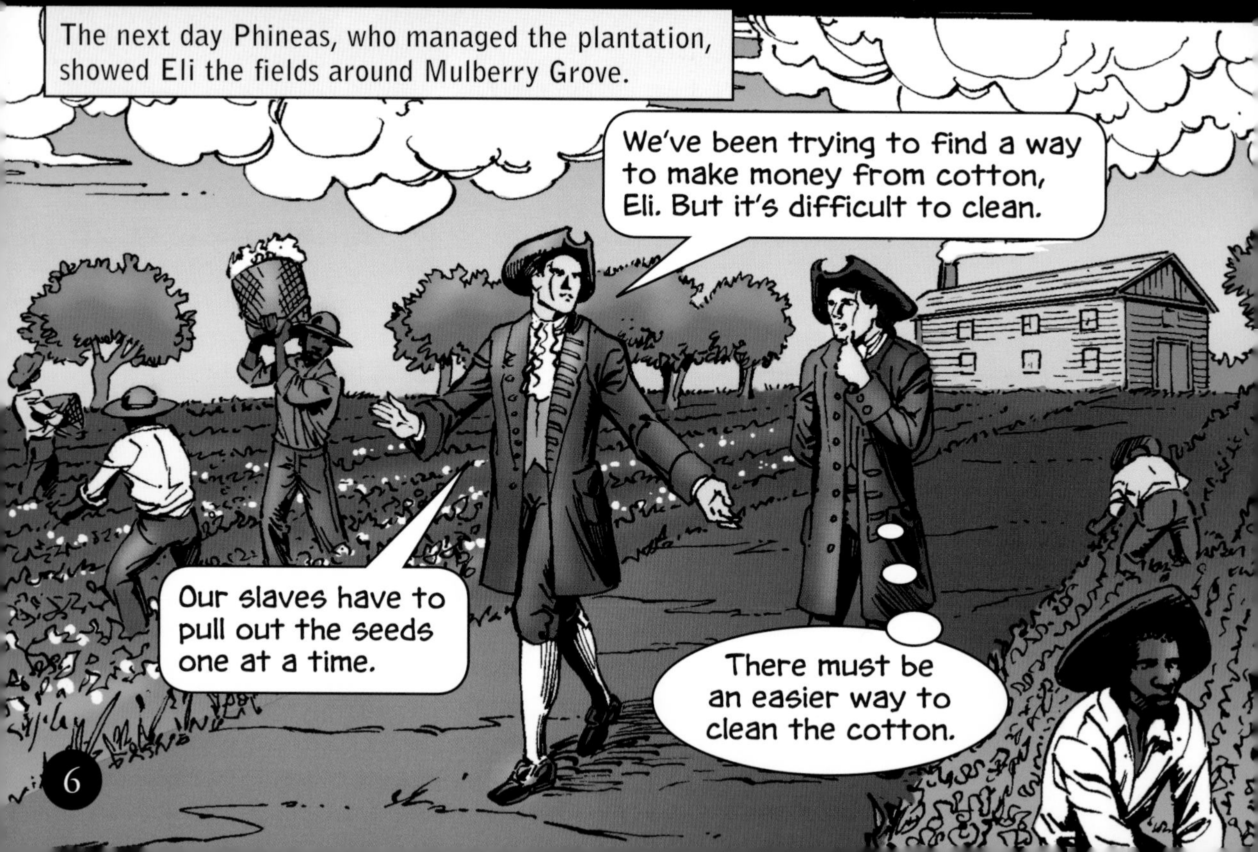
The next day Phineas, who managed the plantation, showed Eli the fields around Mulberry Grove.
We've been trying to find a way to make money from cotton, Eli. But it's difficult to clean.
Our slaves have to pull out the seeds one at a time.
There must be an easier way to clean the cotton.

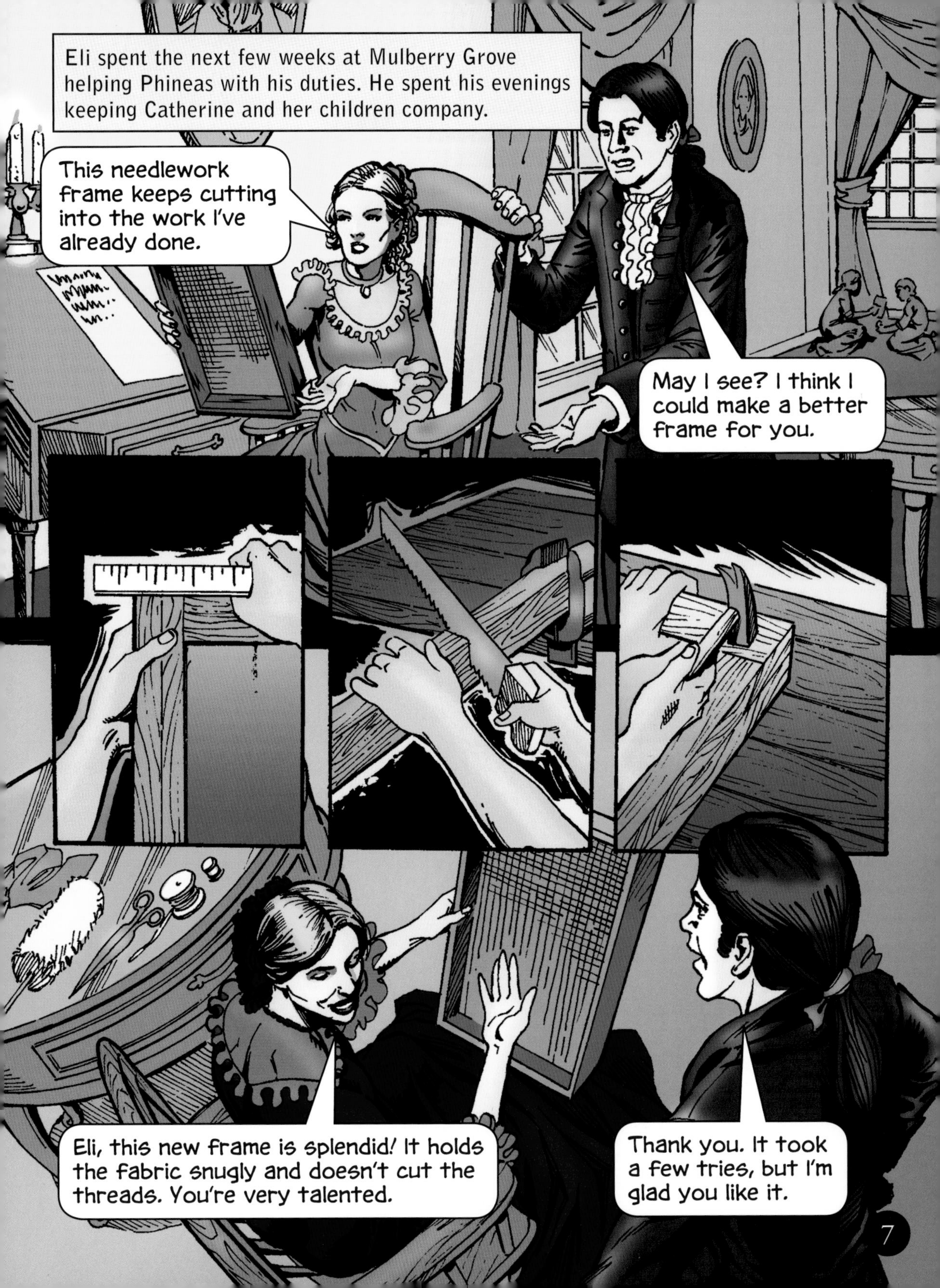

Eli spent the next few weeks at Mulberry Grove helping Phineas with his duties. He spent his evenings keeping Catherine and her children company.
This needlework frame keeps cutting into the work I've already done.
May I see? I think I could make a better frame for you.
Eli, this new frame is splendid! It holds the fabric snugly and doesn't cut the threads. You're very talented.
Thank you. It took a few tries, but I'm glad you like it.

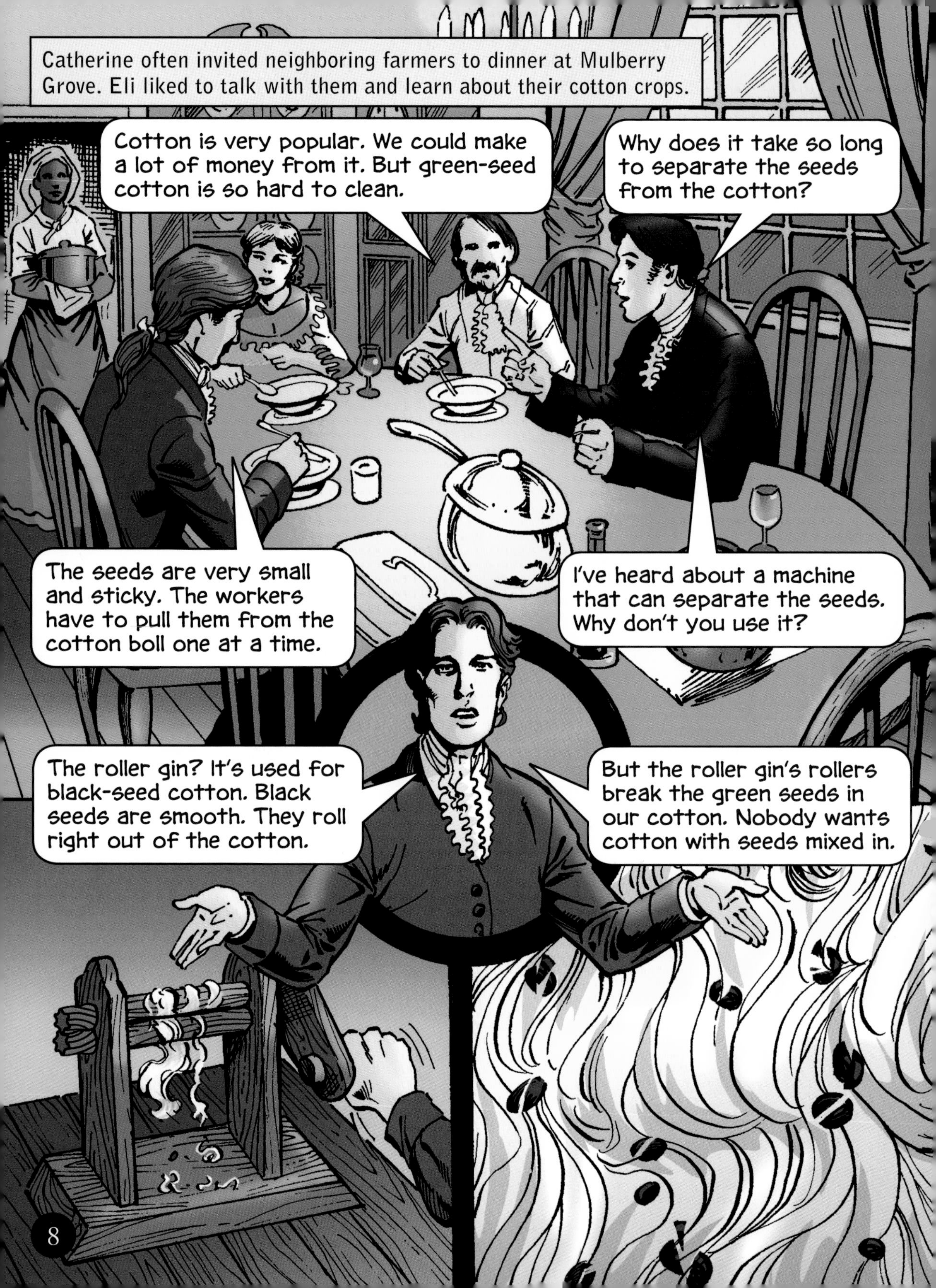
Catherine often invited neighboring farmers to dinner at Mulberry Grove. Eli liked to talk with them and learn about their cotton crops.
Cotton is very popular. We could make a lot of money from it. But green-seed cotton is so hard to clean.
Why does it take so long to separate the seeds from the cotton?
The seeds are very small and sticky. The workers have to pull them from the cotton boll one at a time.
I've heard about a machine that can separate the seeds. Why don't you use it?
The roller gin? It's used for black-seed cotton. Black seeds are smooth. They roll right out of the cotton.
But the roller gin's rollers break the green seeds in our cotton. Nobody wants cotton with seeds mixed in.

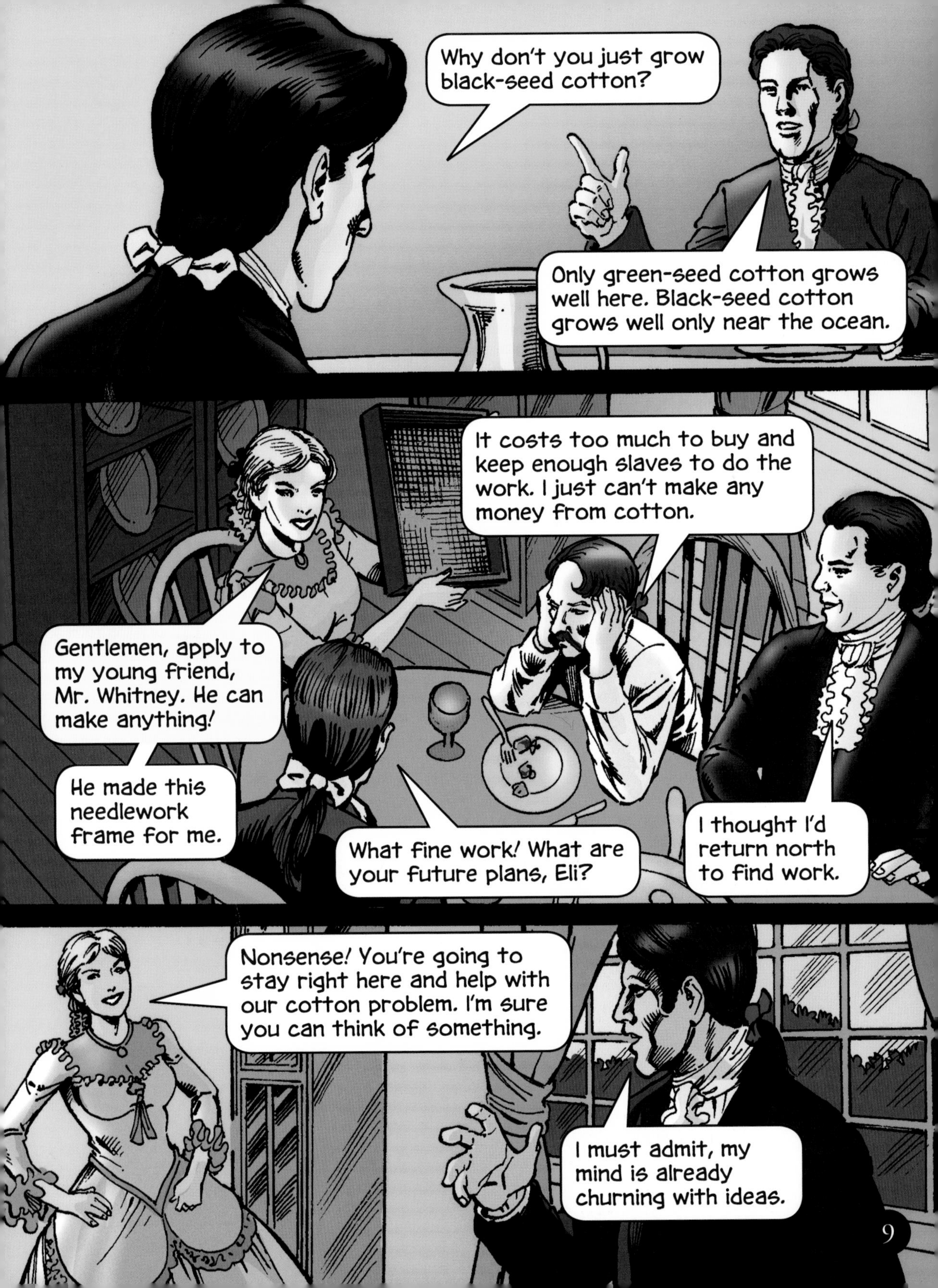
Why don't you just grow black-seed cotton?
Only green-seed cotton grows well here. Black-seed cotton grows well only near the ocean.
It costs too much to buy and keep enough slaves to do the work. I just can't make any money from cotton.
Gentlemen, apply to my young friend, Mr. Whitney. He can make anything!
He made this needlework frame for me.
What fine work! What are your future plans, Eli?
I thought I'd return north to find work.
Nonsense! You're going to stay right here and help with our cotton problem. I'm sure you can think of something.
I must admit, my mind is already churning with ideas.

# Chapter 2
# The Cotton Gin is Born

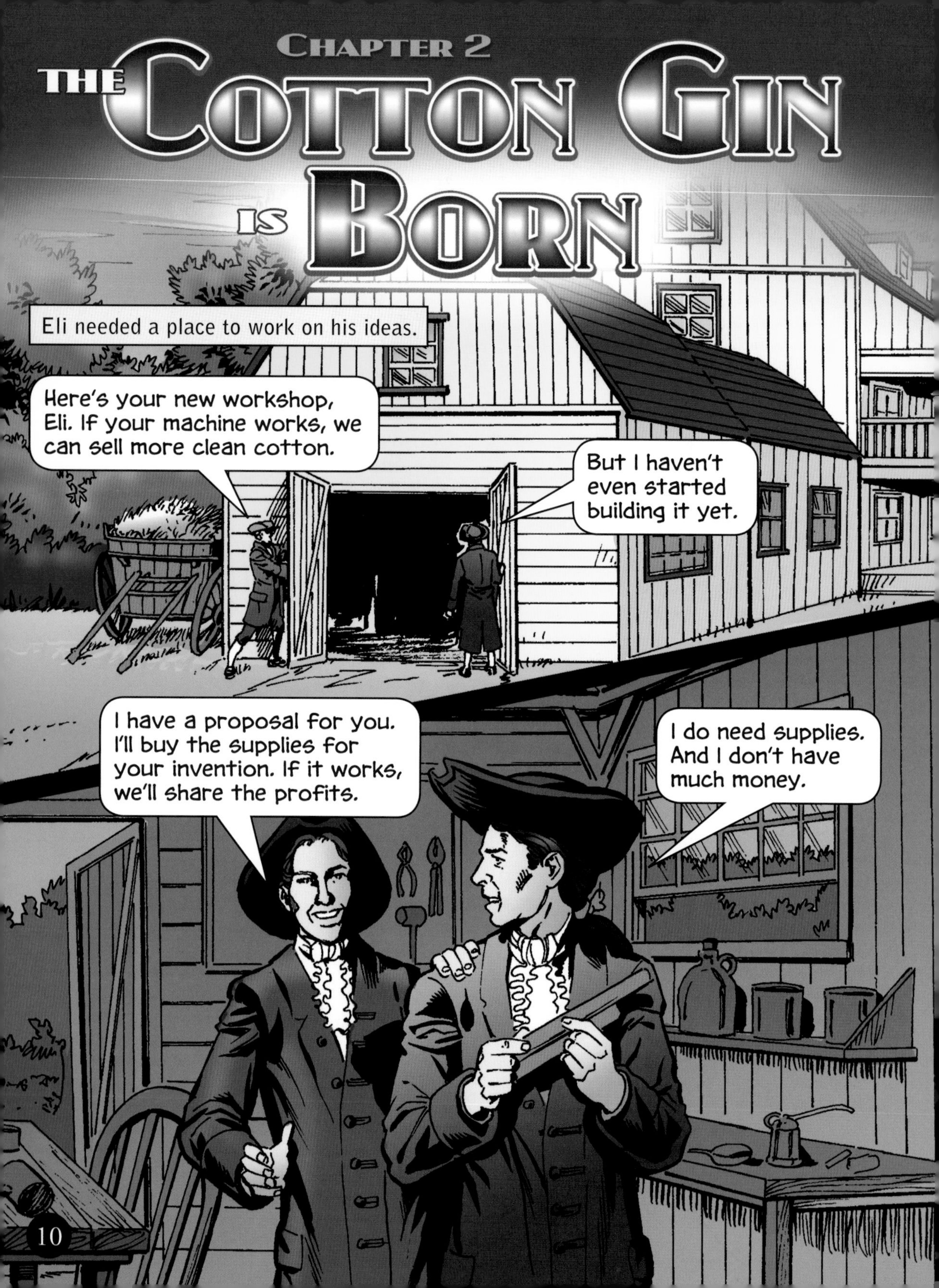
Eli needed a place to work on his ideas.
Here's your new workshop, Eli. If your machine works, we can sell more clean cotton.
But I haven't even started building it yet.
I have a proposal for you. I'll buy the supplies for your invention. If it works, we'll share the profits.
I do need supplies. And I don't have much money.

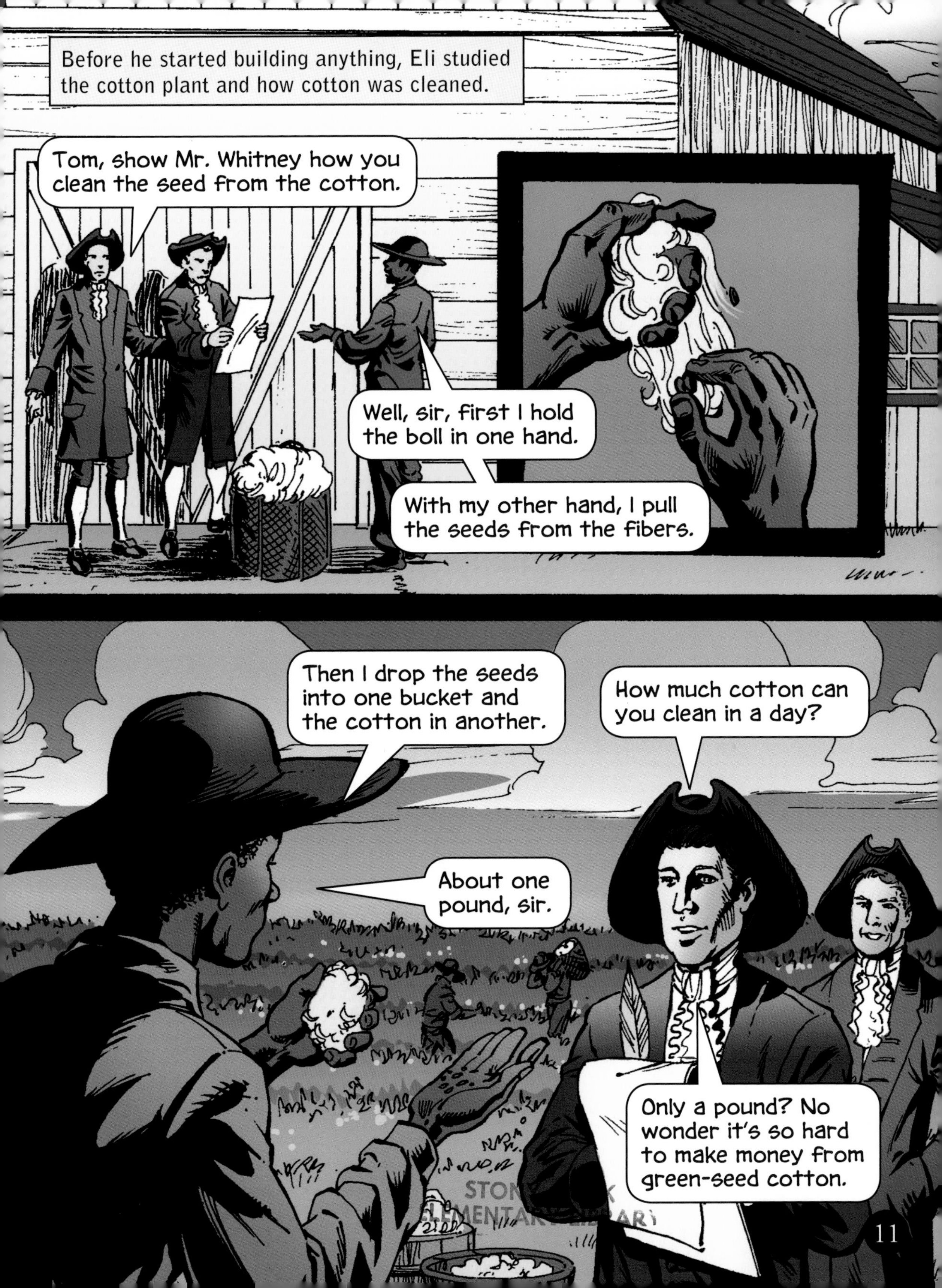
Before he started building anything, Eli studied the cotton plant and how cotton was cleaned.
Tom, show Mr. Whitney how you clean the seed from the cotton.
Well, sir, first I hold the boll in one hand.
With my other hand, I pull the seeds from the fibers.
Then I drop the seeds into one bucket and the cotton in another.
How much cotton can you clean in a day?
About one pound, sir.
Only a pound? No wonder it's so hard to make money from green-seed cotton.

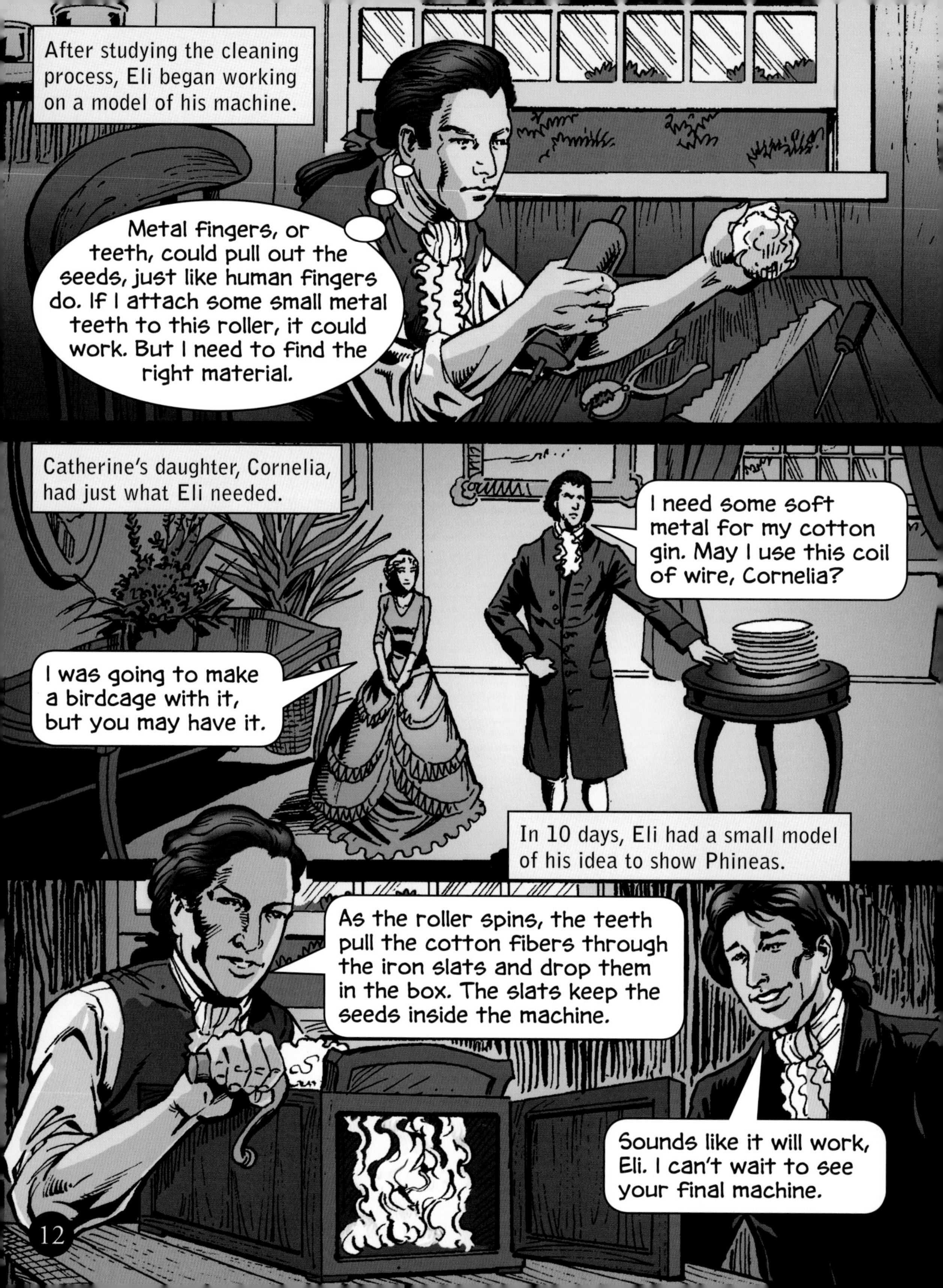
After studying the cleaning process, Eli began working on a model of his machine.
Metal fingers, or teeth, could pull out the seeds, just like human fingers do. If I attach some small metal teeth to this roller, it could work. But I need to find the right material.
Catherine's daughter, Cornelia, had just what Eli needed.
I need some soft metal for my cotton gin. May I use this coil of wire, Cornelia?
I was going to make a birdcage with it, but you may have it.
In 10 days, Eli had a small model of his idea to show Phineas.
As the roller spins, the teeth pull the cotton fibers through the iron slats and drop them in the box. The slats keep the seeds inside the machine.
Sounds like it will work, Eli. I can't wait to see your final machine.

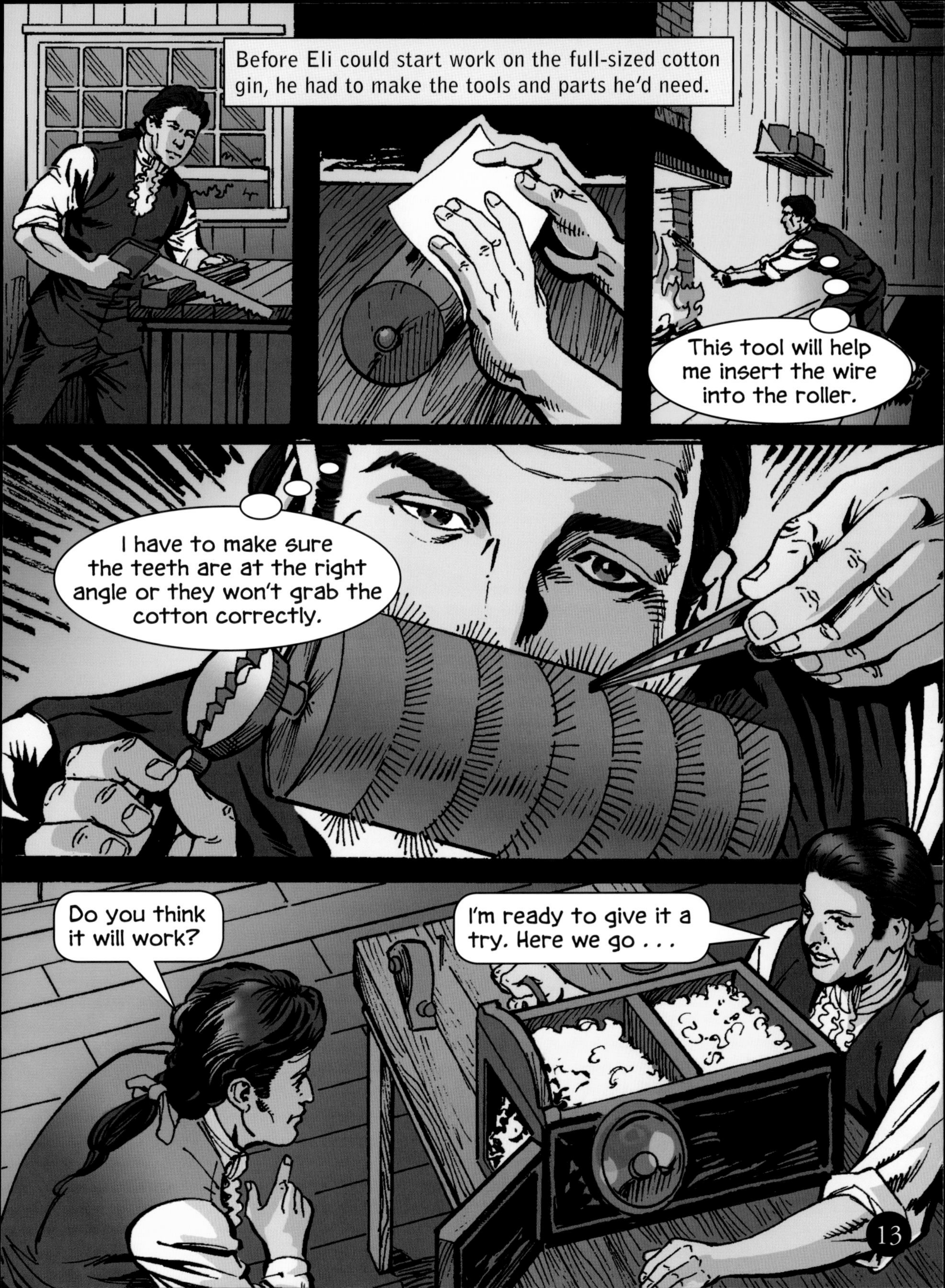
Before Eli could start work on the full-sized cotton gin, he had to make the tools and parts he'd need.
This tool will help me insert the wire into the roller.
I have to make sure the teeth are at the right angle or they won't grab the cotton correctly.
Do you think it will work?
I'm ready to give it a try. Here we go . . .

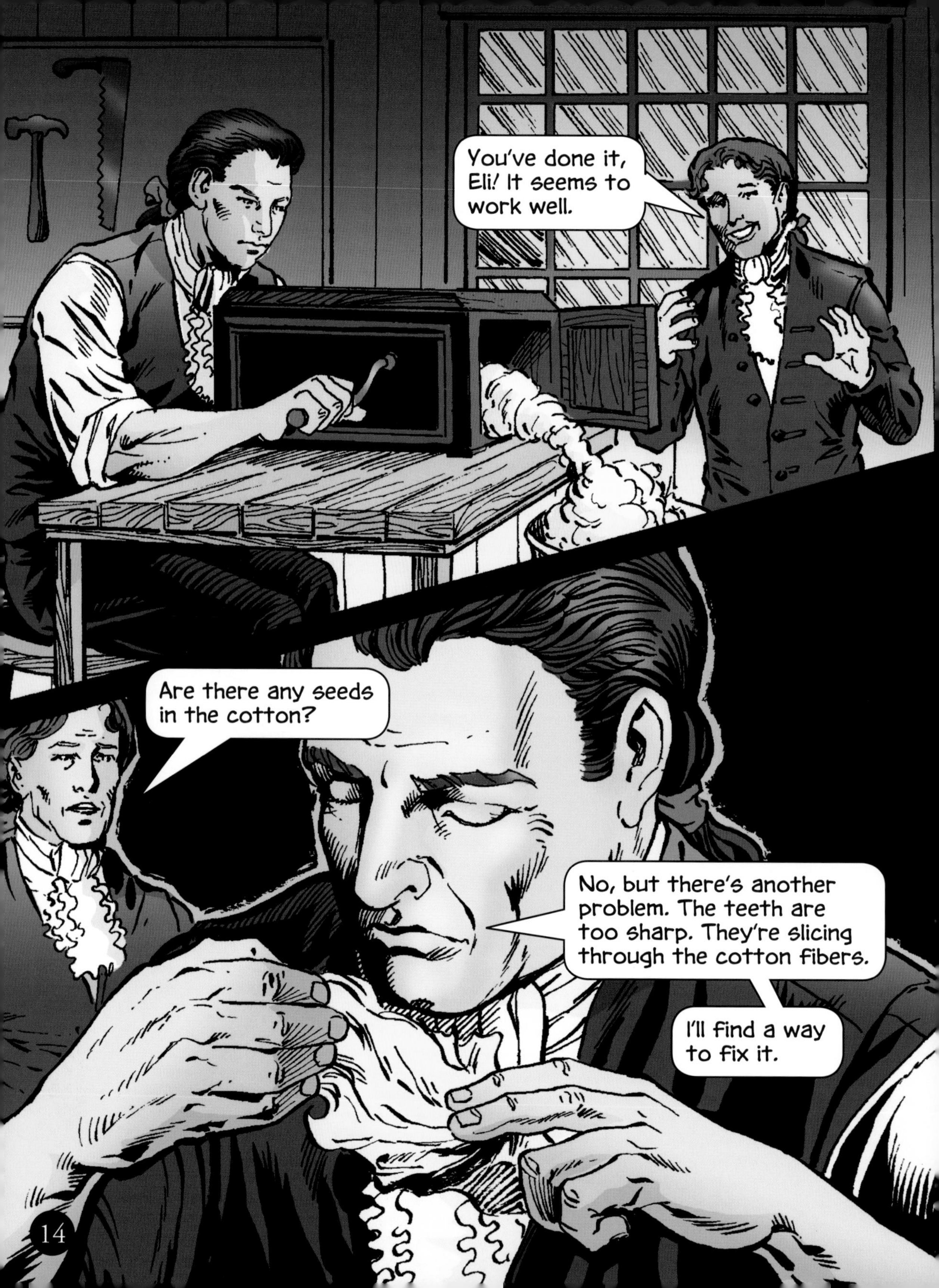
You've done it, Eli! It seems to work well.
Are there any seeds in the cotton?
No, but there's another problem. The teeth are too sharp. They're slicing through the cotton fibers.
I'll find a way to fix it.

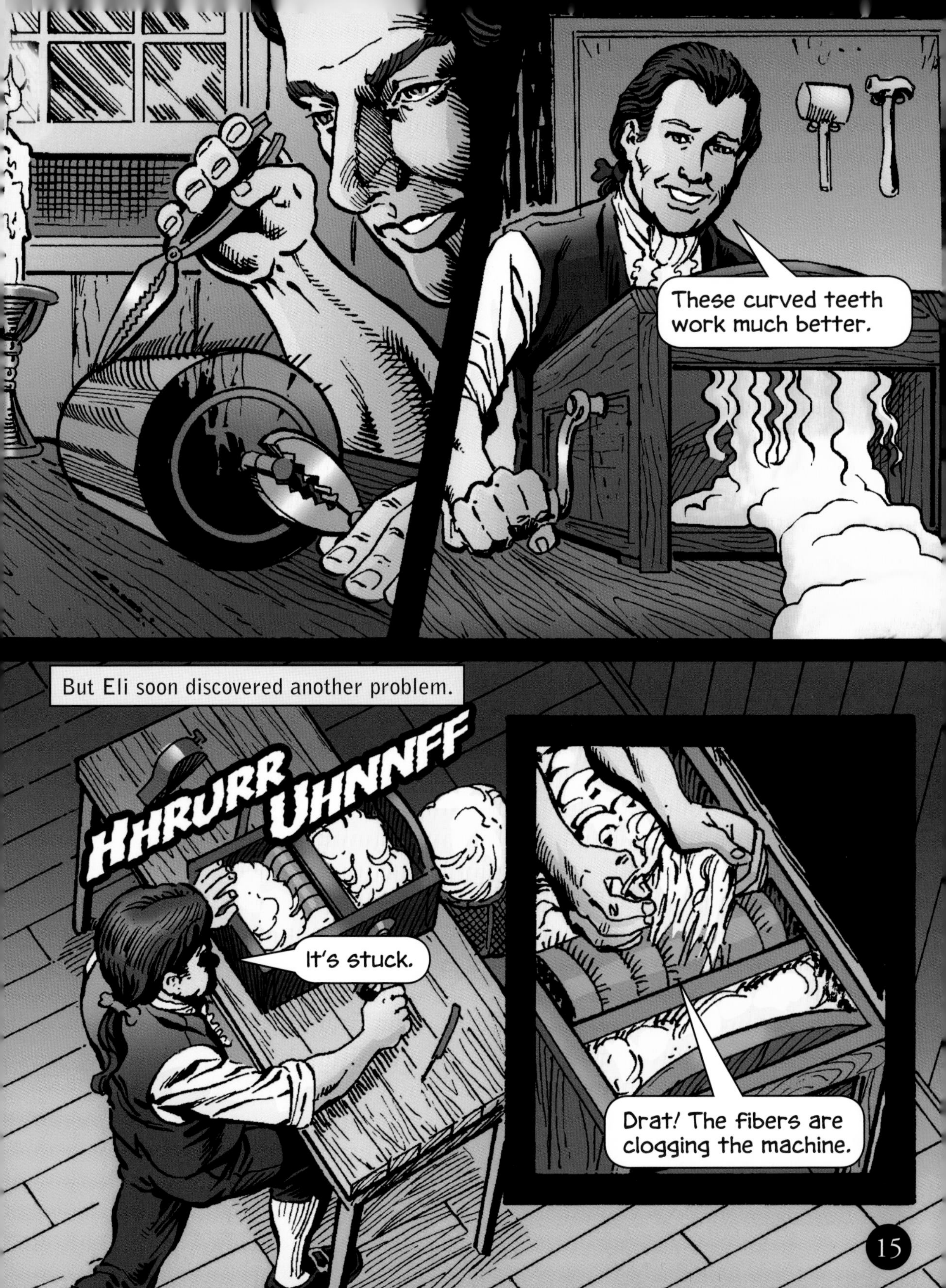
These curved teeth work much better.
But Eli soon discovered another problem.
HHRURR
UHNNFF
It's stuck.
Drat! The fibers are clogging the machine.

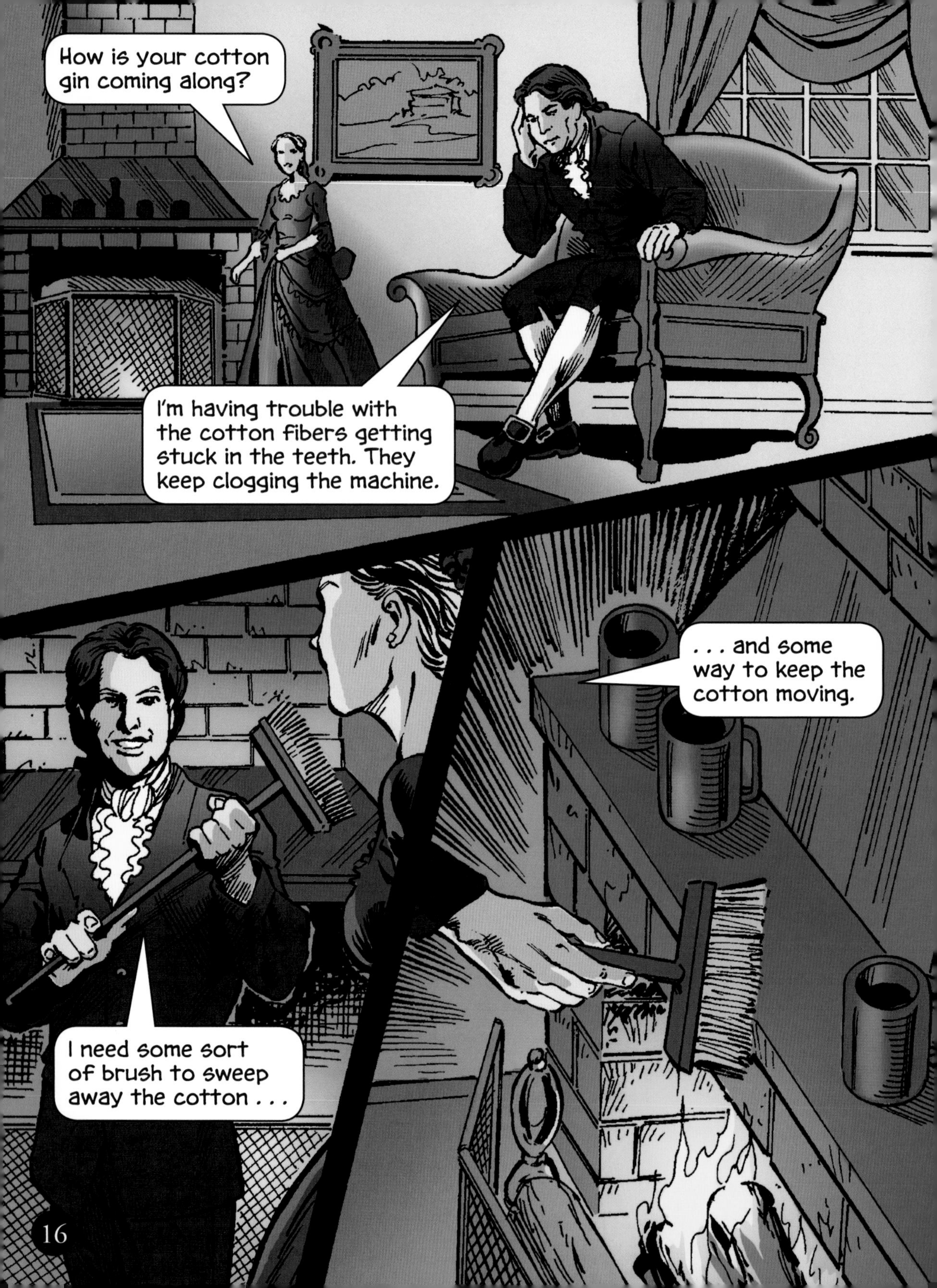
How is your cotton gin coming along?
I'm having trouble with the cotton fibers getting stuck in the teeth. They keep clogging the machine.
I need some sort of brush to sweep away the cotton . . .
. . . and some way to keep the cotton moving.

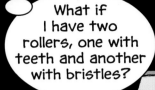

What if I have two rollers, one with teeth and another with bristles?

If I'm right, this brush should clean the cotton from the teeth and drop it into the box.

The next day, Eli showed Phineas his solution.

The brush keeps the roller clean so the gin can keep working.

Fantastic, Eli! I think we should go into business together. Your cotton gin will make us rich.

I'll keep working on the gin, and you can take care of the money and supplies.

Good! It's settled then. We're partners—Miller and Whitney.

17

# Chapter 3
# A Stolen Idea

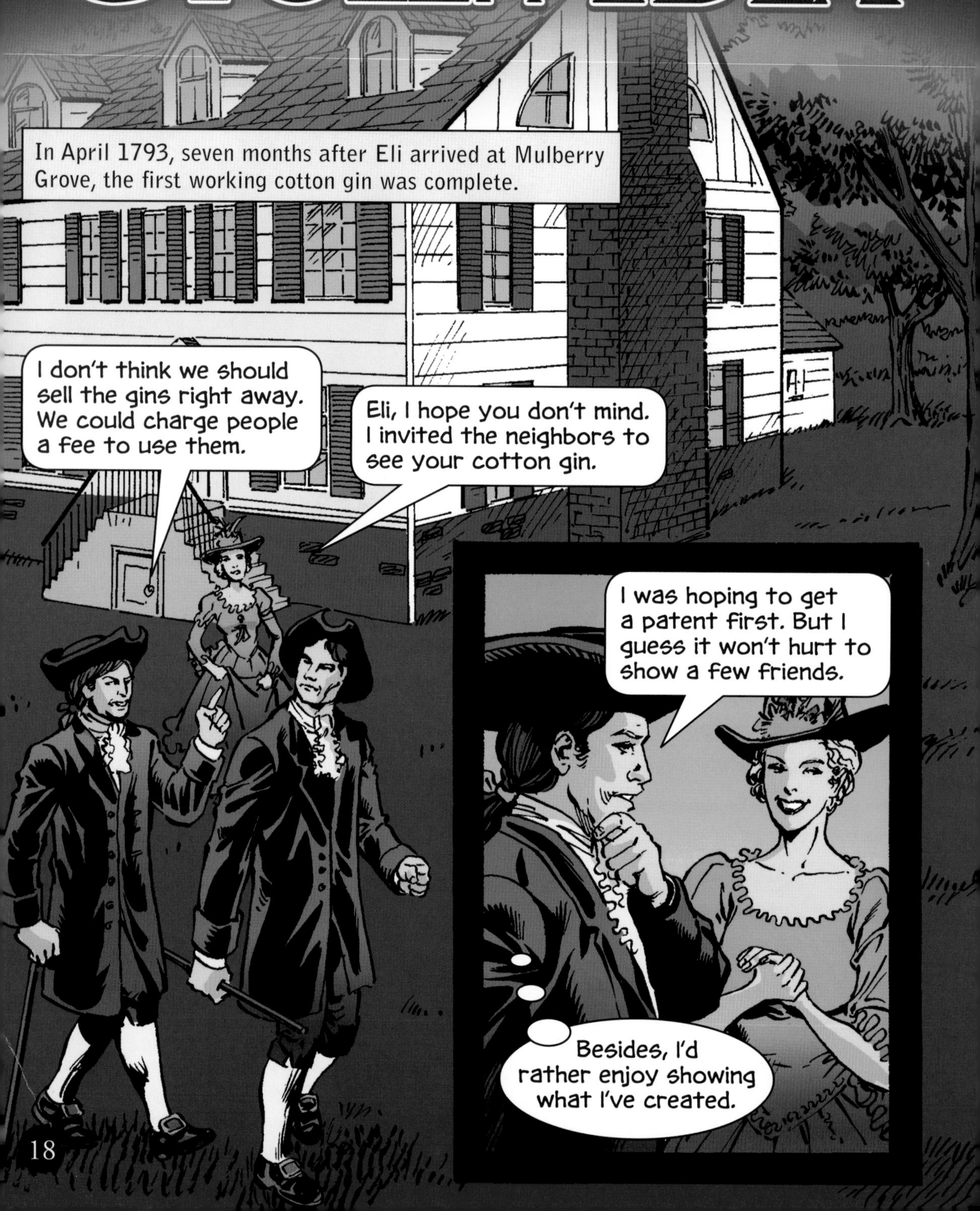

In April 1793, seven months after Eli arrived at Mulberry Grove, the first working cotton gin was complete.
Eli, I hope you don't mind. I invited the neighbors to see your cotton gin.
I don't think we should sell the gins right away. We could charge people a fee to use them.
I was hoping to get a patent first. But I guess it won't hurt to show a few friends.
Besides, I'd rather enjoy showing what I've created.

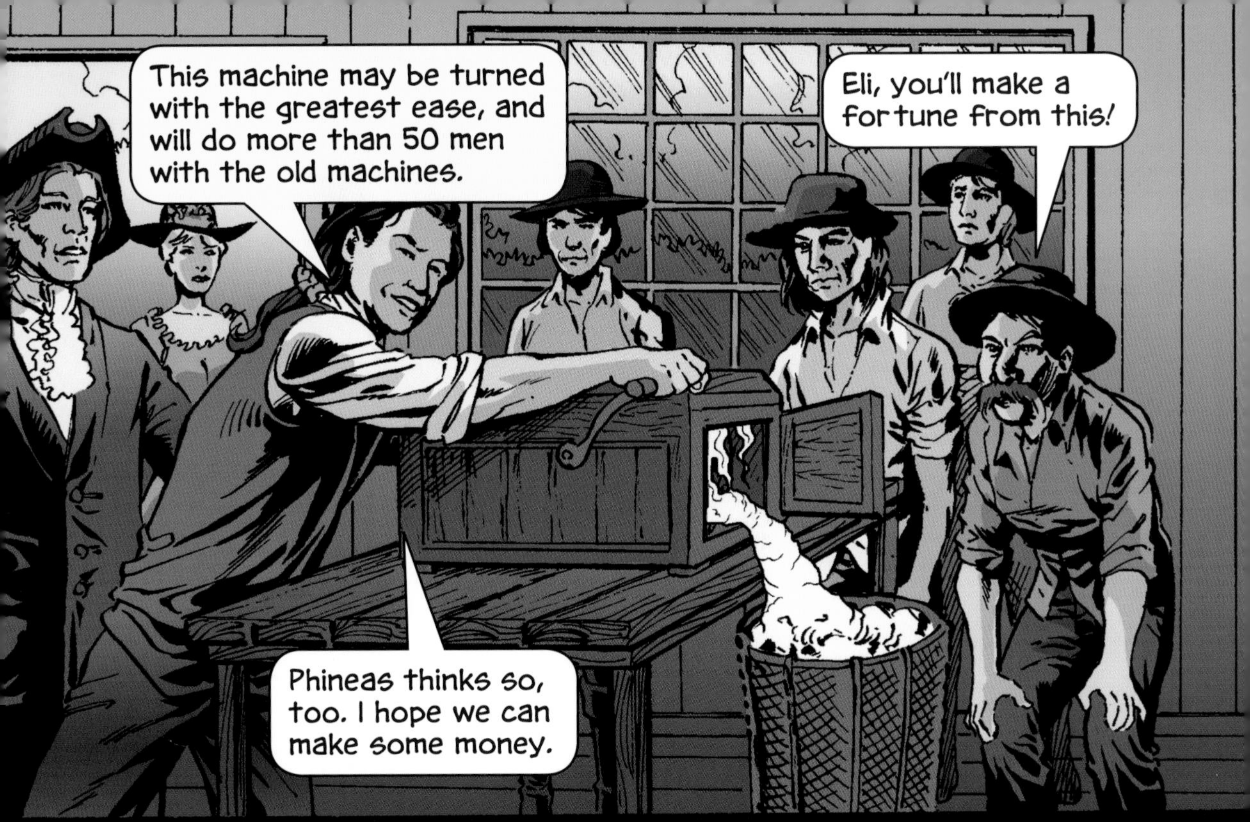
This machine may be turned with the greatest ease, and will do more than 50 men with the old machines.
Eli, you'll make a fortune from this!
Phineas thinks so, too. I hope we can make some money.

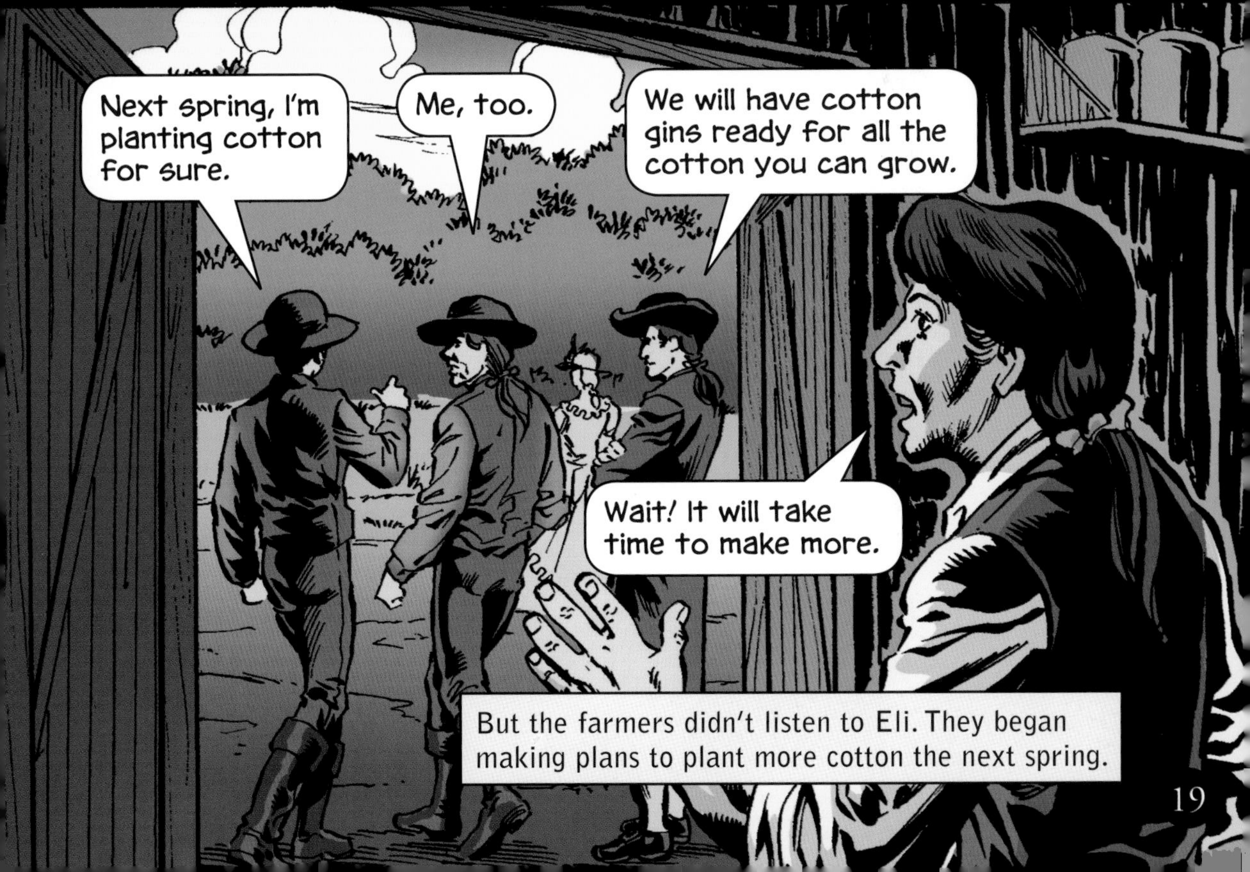
Next spring, I'm planting cotton for sure.
Me, too.
We will have cotton gins ready for all the cotton you can grow.
Wait! It will take time to make more.
But the farmers didn't listen to Eli. They began making plans to plant more cotton the next spring.

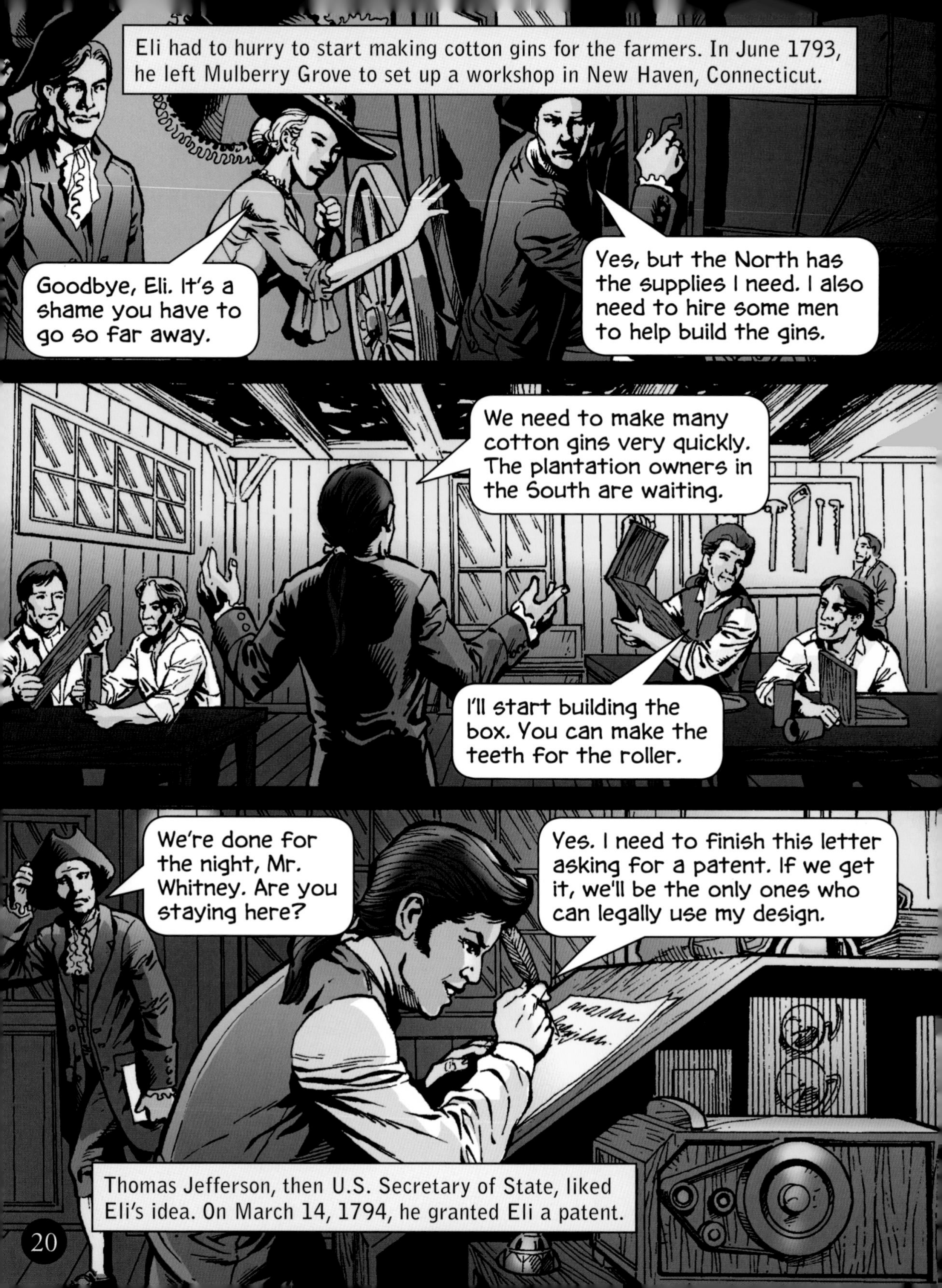
Eli had to hurry to start making cotton gins for the farmers. In June 1793, he left Mulberry Grove to set up a workshop in New Haven, Connecticut.
Goodbye, Eli. It's a shame you have to go so far away.
Yes, but the North has the supplies I need. I also need to hire some men to help build the gins.
We need to make many cotton gins very quickly. The plantation owners in the South are waiting.
I'll start building the box. You can make the teeth for the roller.
We're done for the night, Mr. Whitney. Are you staying here?
Yes. I need to finish this letter asking for a patent. If we get it, we'll be the only ones who can legally use my design.
Thomas Jefferson, then U.S. Secretary of State, liked Eli's idea. On March 14, 1794, he granted Eli a patent.

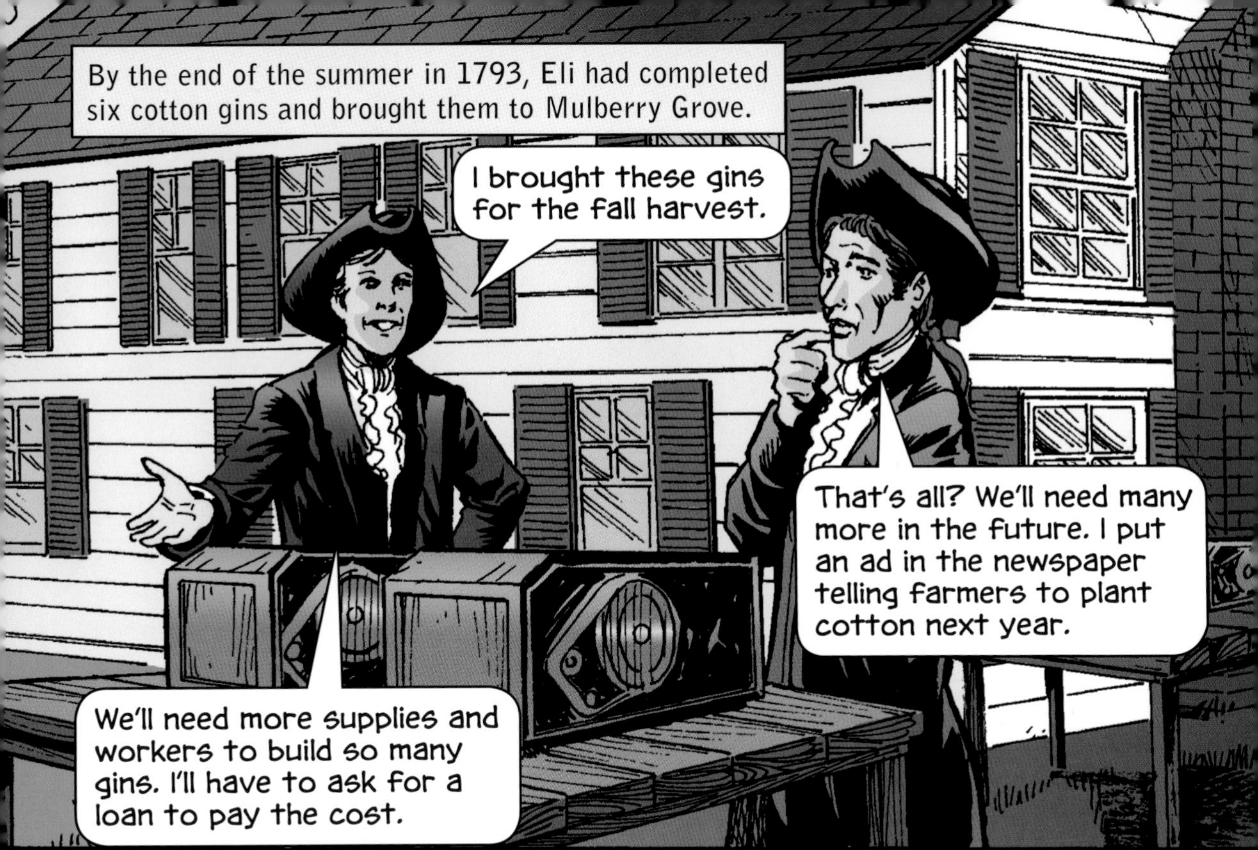
By the end of the summer in 1793, Eli had completed six cotton gins and brought them to Mulberry Grove.
I brought these gins for the fall harvest.
That's all? We'll need many more in the future. I put an ad in the newspaper telling farmers to plant cotton next year.
We'll need more supplies and workers to build so many gins. I'll have to ask for a loan to pay the cost.

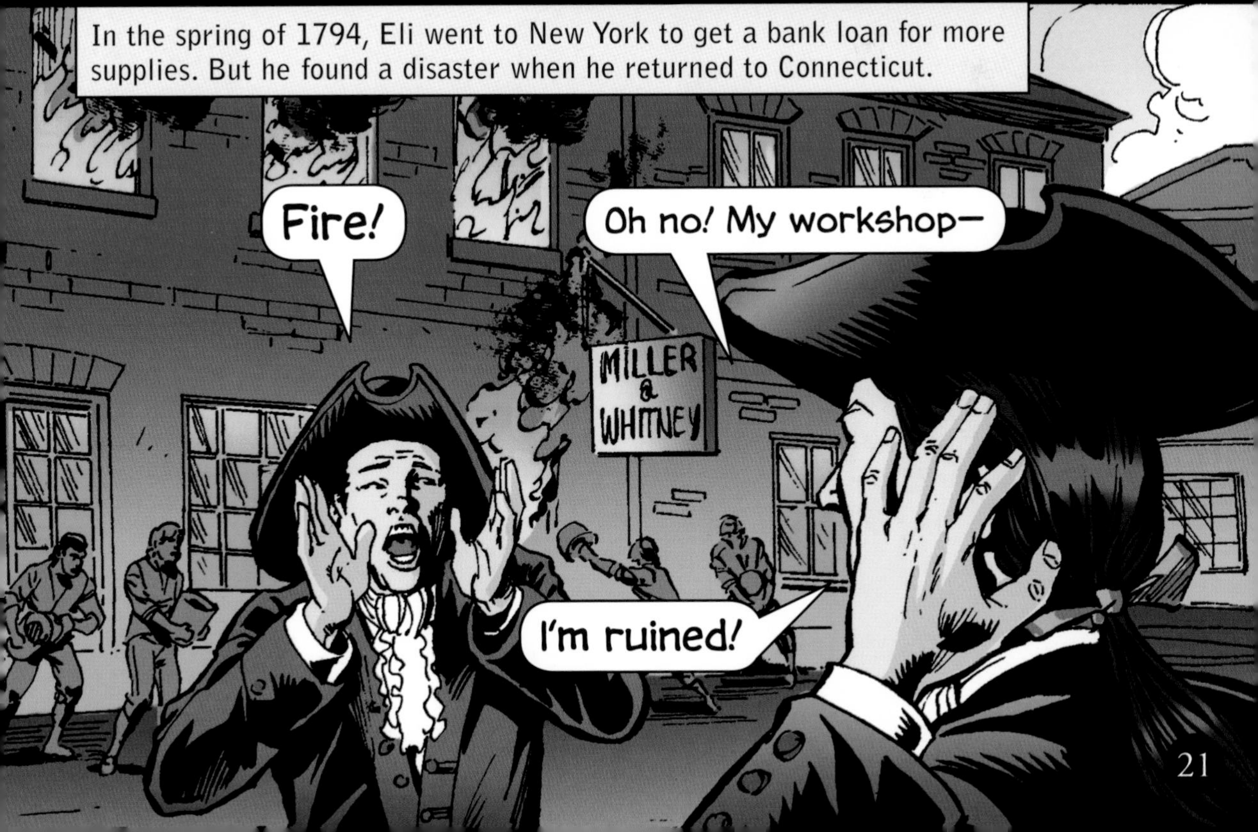
In the spring of 1794, Eli went to New York to get a bank loan for more supplies. But he found a disaster when he returned to Connecticut.
Fire!
Oh no! My workshop—
MILLER & WHITNEY
I'm ruined!

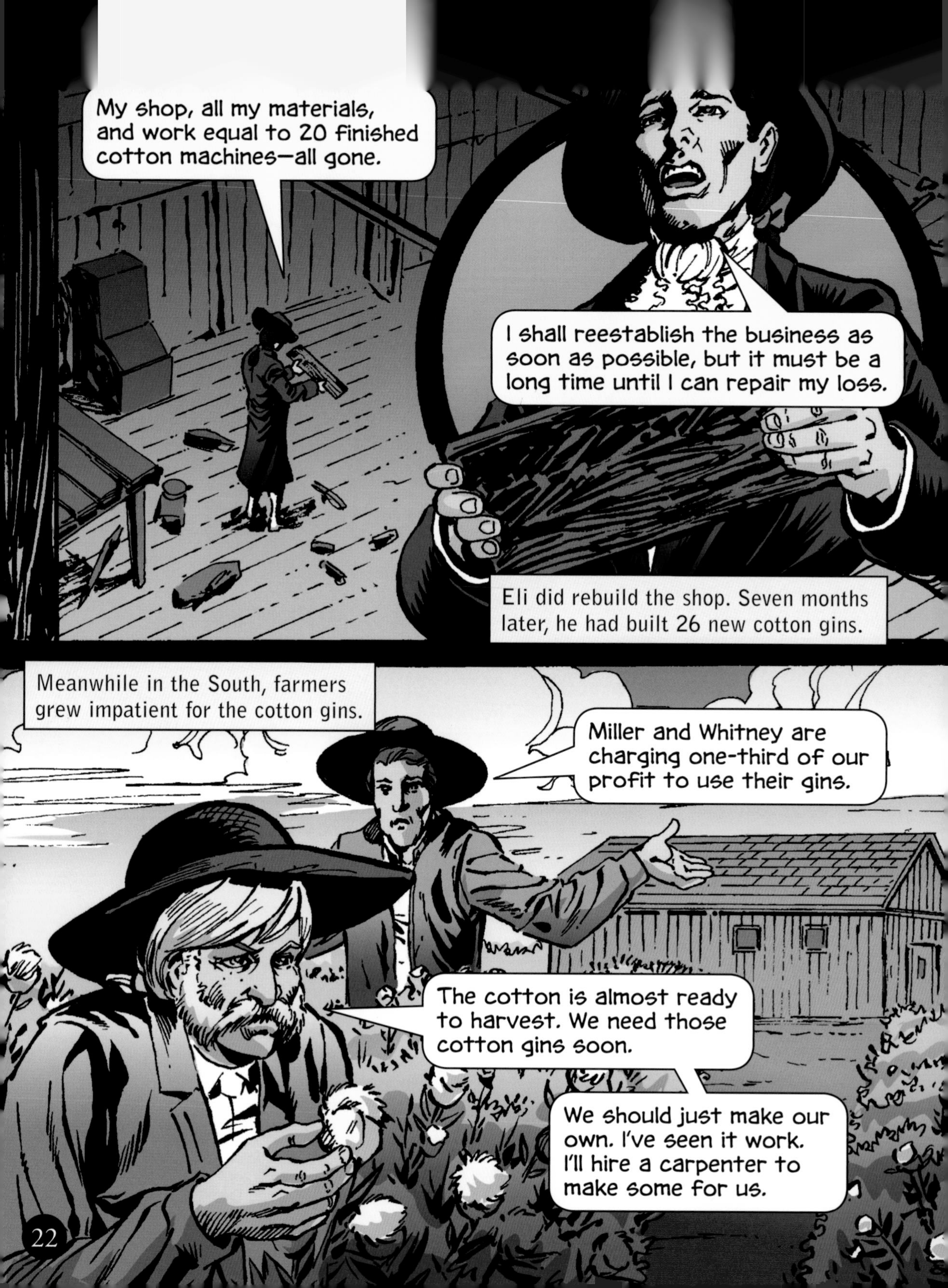
My shop, all my materials, and work equal to 20 finished cotton machines—all gone.
I shall reestablish the business as soon as possible, but it must be a long time until I can repair my loss.
Eli did rebuild the shop. Seven months later, he had built 26 new cotton gins.
Meanwhile in the South, farmers grew impatient for the cotton gins.
Miller and Whitney are charging one-third of our profit to use their gins.
The cotton is almost ready to harvest. We need those cotton gins soon.
We should just make our own. I've seen it work. I'll hire a carpenter to make some for us.

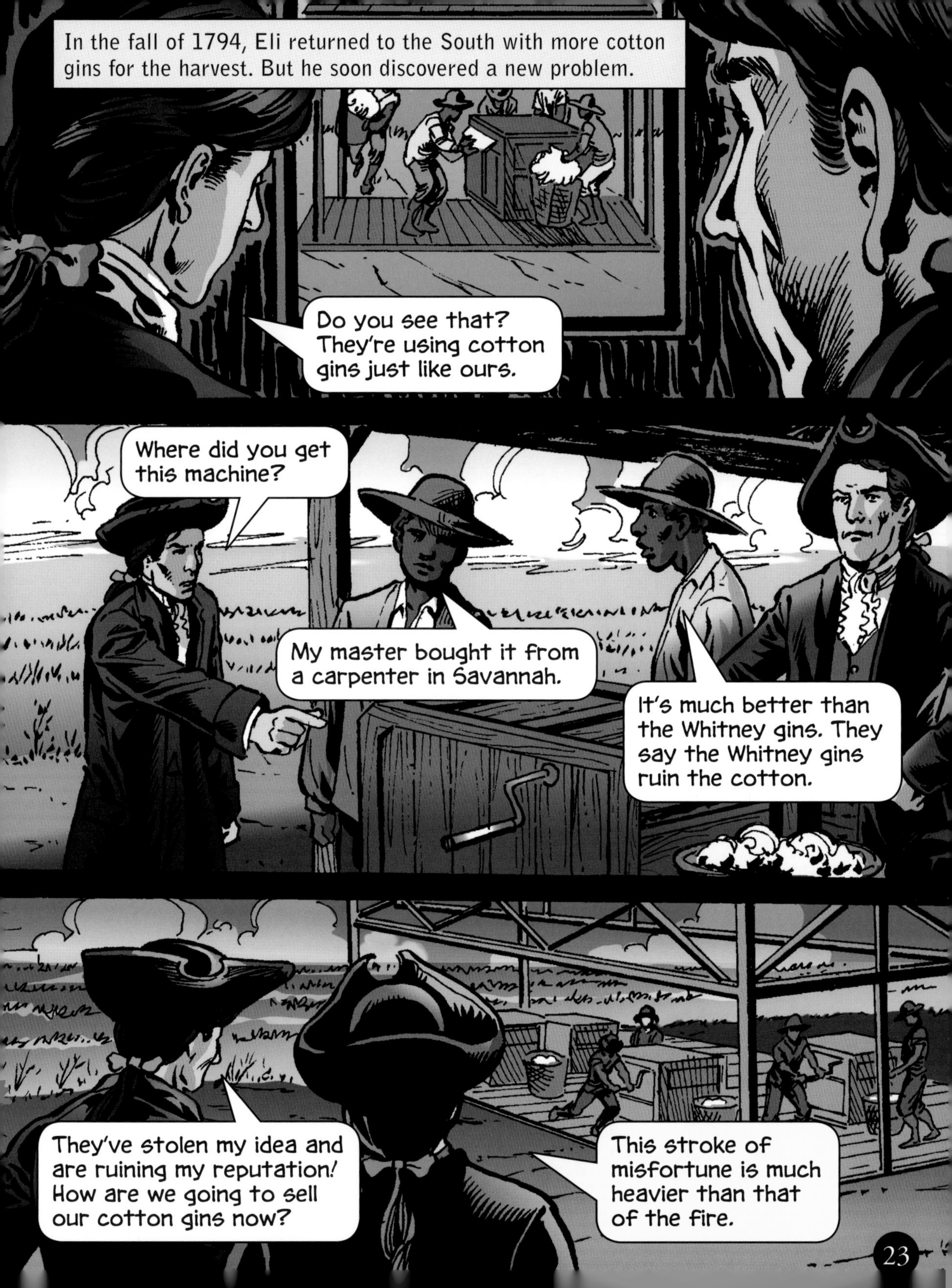
In the fall of 1794, Eli returned to the South with more cotton gins for the harvest. But he soon discovered a new problem.
Do you see that? They're using cotton gins just like ours.
Where did you get this machine?
My master bought it from a carpenter in Savannah.
It's much better than the Whitney gins. They say the Whitney gins ruin the cotton.
They've stolen my idea and are ruining my reputation! How are we going to sell our cotton gins now?
This stroke of misfortune is much heavier than that of the fire.

# Chapter 4
# The Cost of a Dream

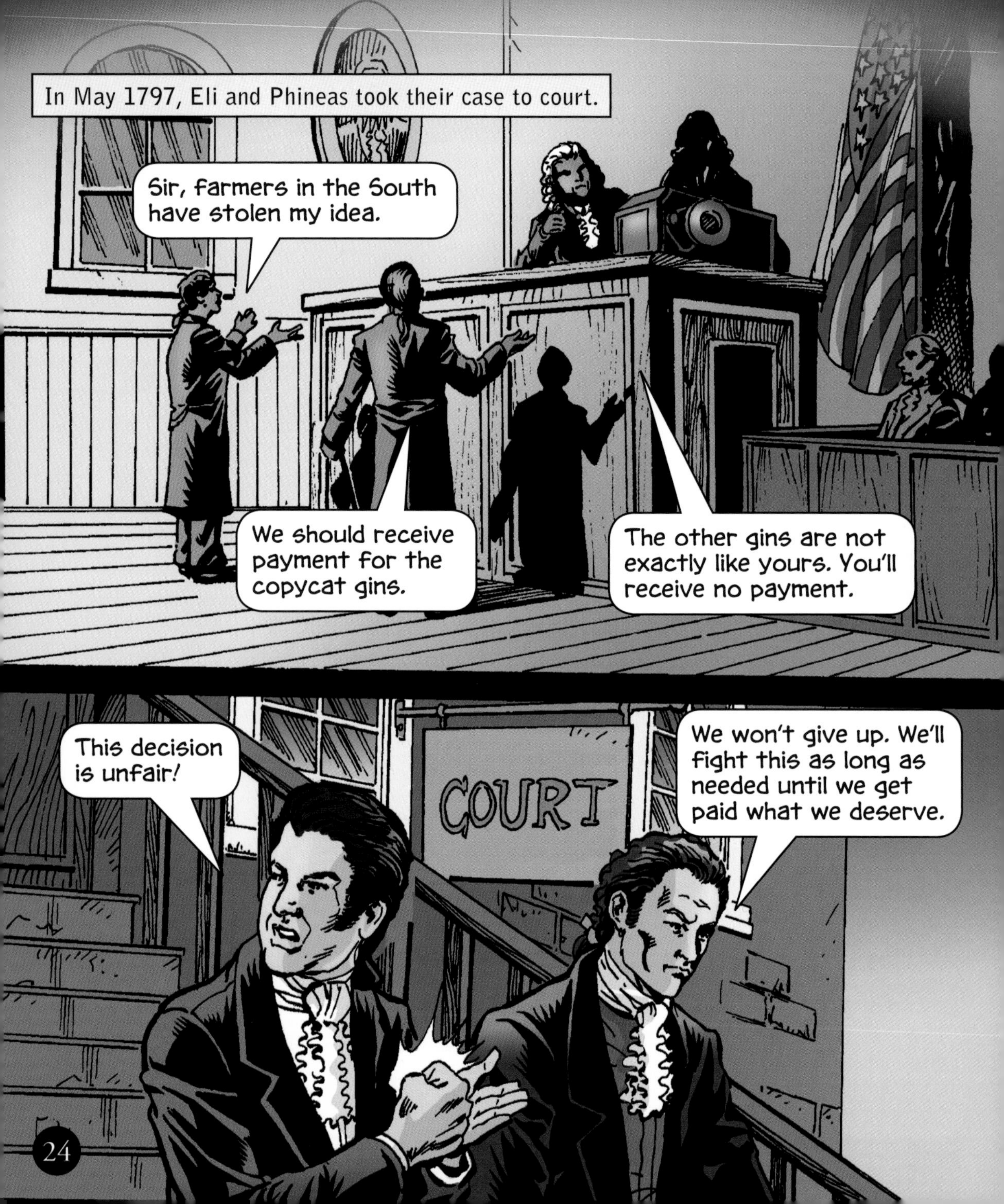
In May 1797, Eli and Phineas took their case to court.
Sir, farmers in the South have stolen my idea.
We should receive payment for the copycat gins.
The other gins are not exactly like yours. You'll receive no payment.
This decision is unfair!
COURT
We won't give up. We'll fight this as long as needed until we get paid what we deserve.

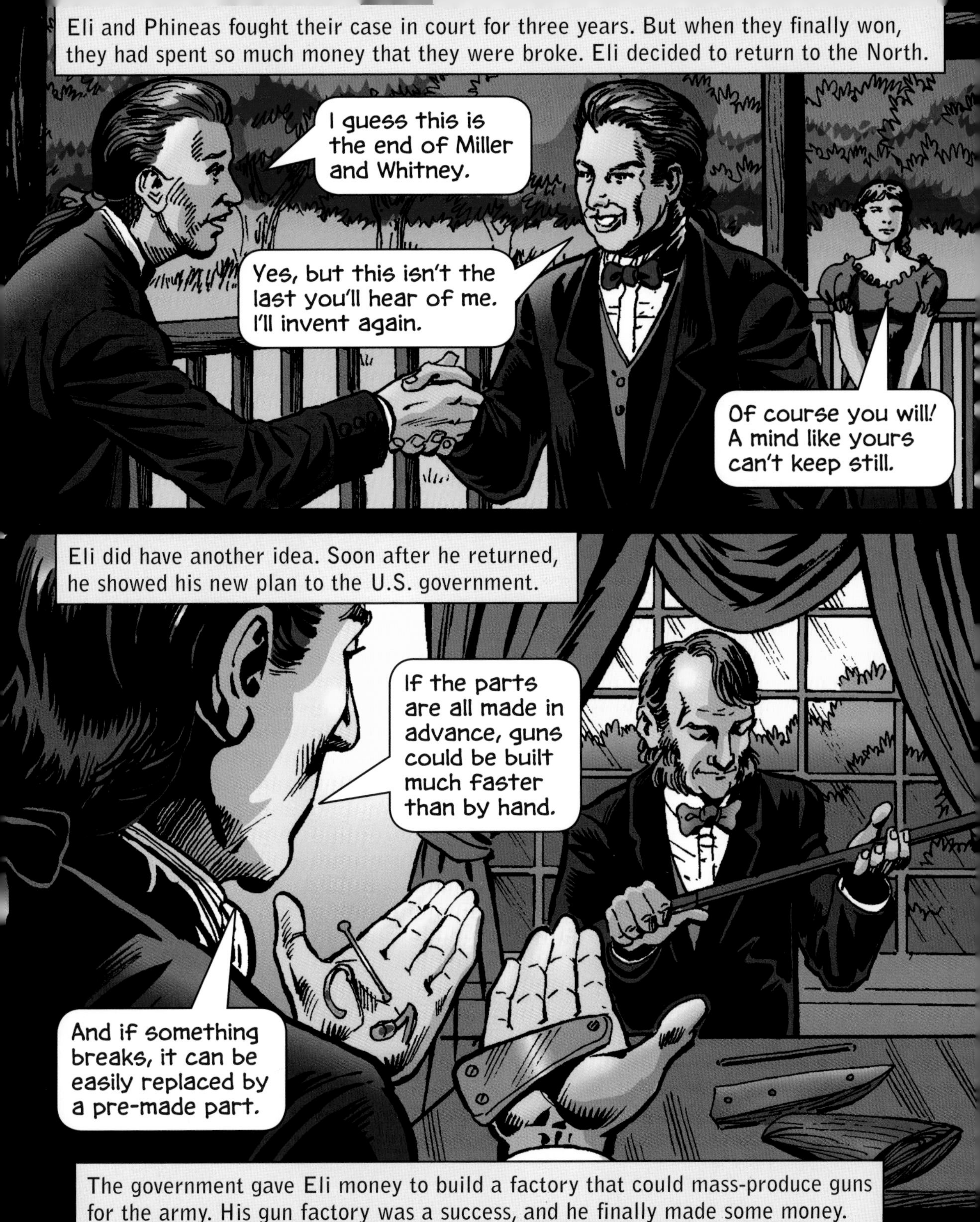
Eli and Phineas fought their case in court for three years. But when they finally won, they had spent so much money that they were broke. Eli decided to return to the North.
I guess this is the end of Miller and Whitney.
Yes, but this isn't the last you'll hear of me. I'll invent again.
Of course you will! A mind like yours can't keep still.
Eli did have another idea. Soon after he returned, he showed his new plan to the U.S. government.
If the parts are all made in advance, guns could be built much faster than by hand.
And if something breaks, it can be easily replaced by a pre-made part.
The government gave Eli money to build a factory that could mass-produce guns for the army. His gun factory was a success, and he finally made some money.

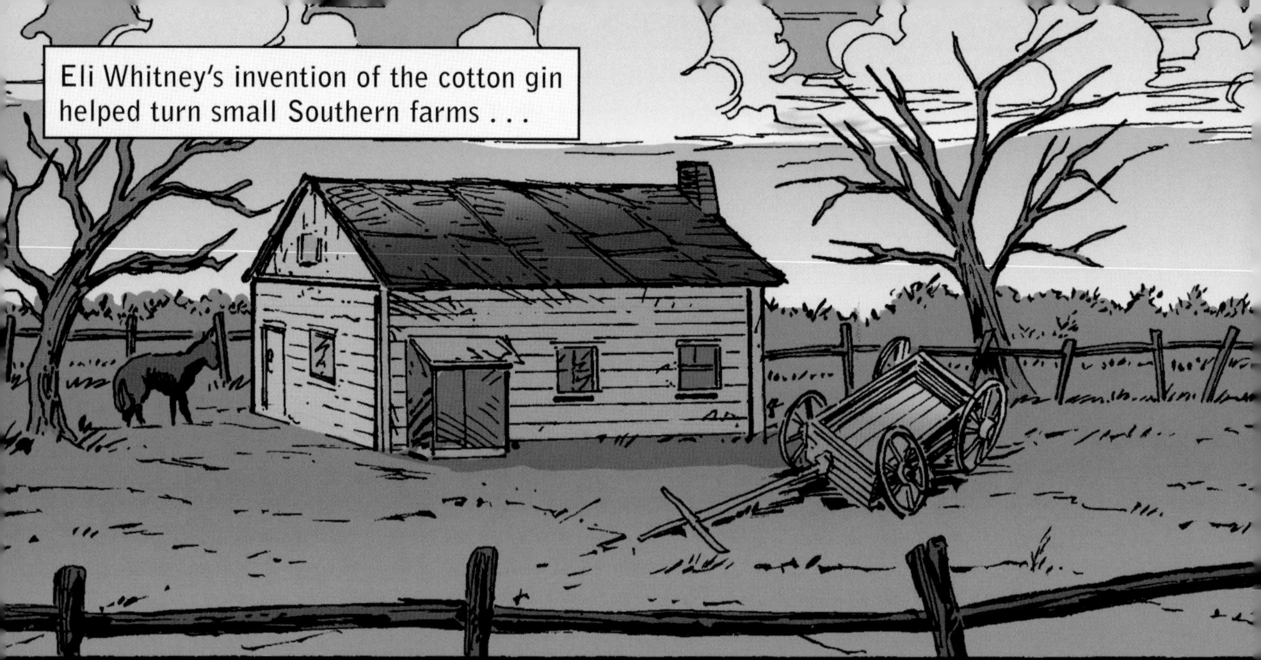
Eli Whitney's invention of the cotton gin helped turn small Southern farms . . .

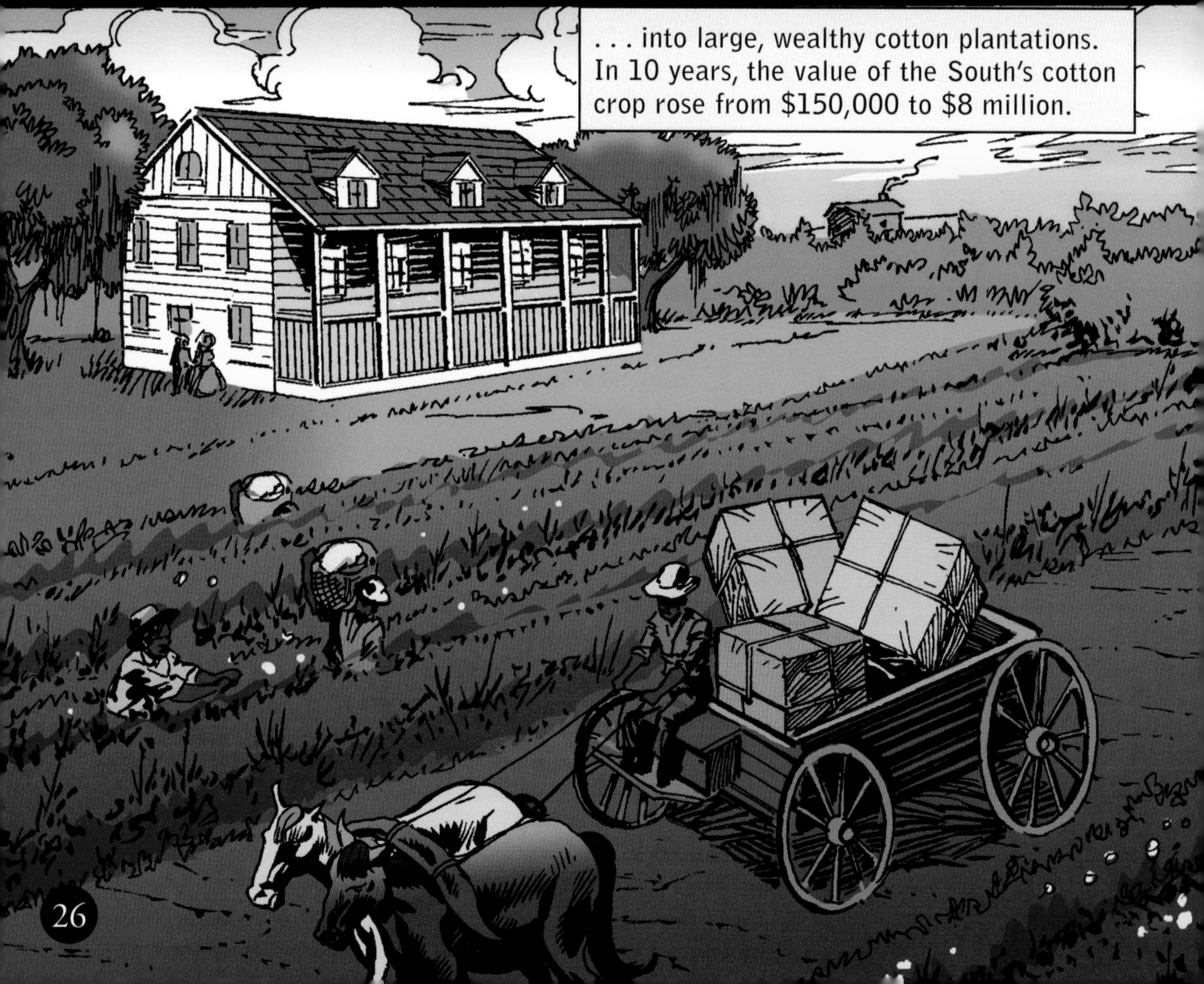
. . . into large, wealthy cotton plantations. In 10 years, the value of the South's cotton crop rose from $150,000 to $8 million.

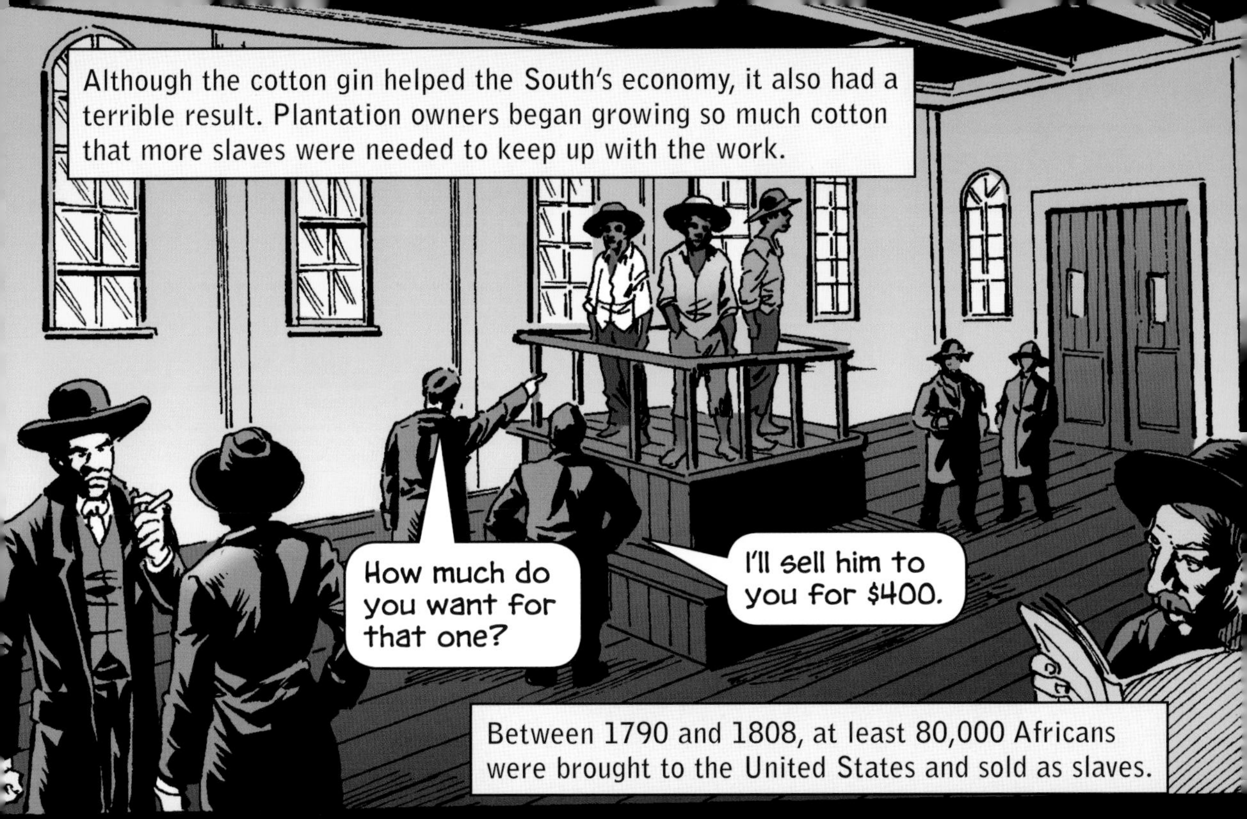
Although the cotton gin helped the South's economy, it also had a terrible result. Plantation owners began growing so much cotton that more slaves were needed to keep up with the work.
How much do you want for that one?
I'll sell him to you for $400.
Between 1790 and 1808, at least 80,000 Africans were brought to the United States and sold as slaves.

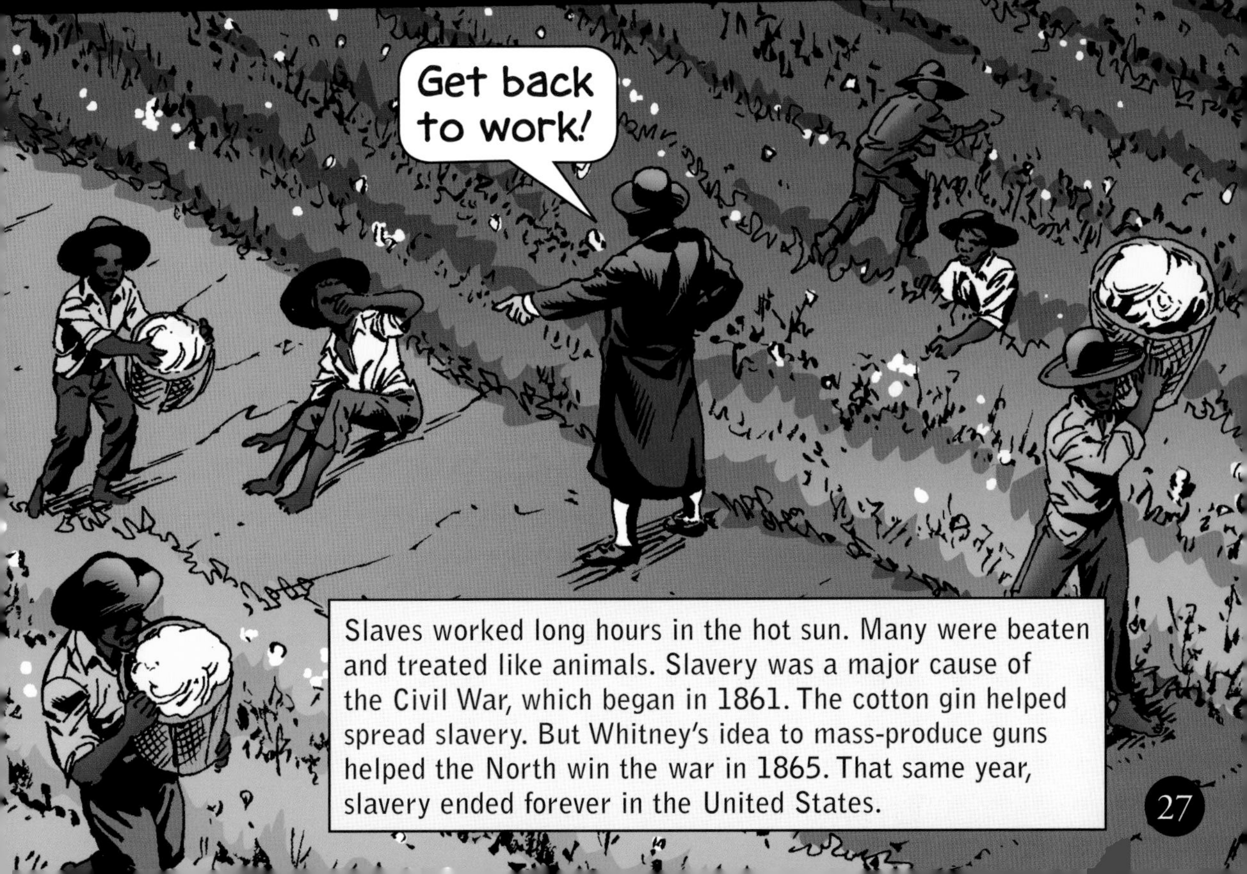
Get back to work!
Slaves worked long hours in the hot sun. Many were beaten and treated like animals. Slavery was a major cause of the Civil War, which began in 1861. The cotton gin helped spread slavery. But Whitney's idea to mass-produce guns helped the North win the war in 1865. That same year, slavery ended forever in the United States.

# MORE ABOUT
# ELI WHITNEY AND THE
# COTTON GIN

 Eli Whitney was born December 8, 1765, in Westborough, Massachusetts. He died January 8, 1825, in New Haven, Connectictut.

 In cotton gin, the word "gin" is short for "engine."

 Hodgen Holmes made cotton gins similar to Eli Whitney's. Holmes used a saw instead of wire teeth in his cotton gin. Because he used a saw, the courts ruled that it was a different invention, not a stolen one.

 After their legal battles, Eli and Phineas decided to sell the cotton gins instead of charging farmers to use them. The farmers were satisfied with this idea and bought many of the cotton gins.

 Phineas Miller and Catherine Greene were married in 1796. They had so many financial troubles that they had to sell the plantation in 1800. Mulberry Grove sold for only $15,000.

The ability to easily clean green-seed cotton with the cotton gin caused slavery to spread in the South. In 1790 there were six slave states. By 1860 there were 15 slave states.

 The cotton gin is still used to clean cotton. Today's cotton gins are similar to Eli Whitney's but use electric motors, rather than men or horses, to power them.

 Clothing is not the only cotton product. Cotton is also used in blankets, tents, and even dollar bills. Cottonseed oil is used in cooking oil, salad dressing, crackers, and cookies.

 Eli Whitney's idea to use interchangeable parts to mass-produce products is still being used today. From small toys to large machines, almost everything is built using this method.

# GLOSSARY

boll (BOHL)—a round pod on some plants that contains seeds

fiber (FYE-bur)—a long, thin thread of material, such as cotton, wool, or silk

patent (PAT-uhnt)—a legal document giving an inventor sole rights to make and sell an item he or she invented

plantation (plan-TAY-shuhn)—a large farm where one main crop is grown, such as coffee, tobacco, or cotton

profit (PROF-it)—the amount of money left after all the costs of running a business have been subtracted

reestablish (ree-ess-TAB-lish)—to set up again

# INTERNET SITES

FactHound offers a safe, fun way to find Internet sites related to this book. All of the sites on FactHound have been researched by our staff.

Here's how:
1. Visit *www.facthound.com*
2. Choose your grade level.
3. Type in this book ID **0736868437** for age-appropriate sites. You may also browse subjects by clicking on letters, or by clicking on pictures and words.
4. Click on the **Fetch It** button.

**FactHound will fetch the best sites for you!**

# READ MORE

Bagley, Katie. *Eli Whitney: American Inventor.* Let Freedom Ring. Mankato, Minn.: Capstone Press, 2003.

Cefrey, Holly. *The Inventions of Eli Whitney: The Cotton Gin.* 19th Century American Inventors. New York: PowerKids Press, 2003.

Masters, Nancy Robinson. *The Cotton Gin.* Inventions That Shaped the World. New York: Franklin Watts, 2006.

Mitchell, Barbara. *Maker of Machines: A Story About Eli Whitney.* Creative Minds Biography. Minneapolis: Carolrhoda Books, 2004.

# BIBILIOGRAPHY

Britton, Karen G. *Bale O' Cotton: The Mechanical Art of Cotton Ginning.* College Station, Texas: A&M University Press, 1992.

Green, Constance McLaughlin. *Eli Whitney and the Birth of American Technology.* Boston: Little, Brown, 1956.

Iles, George. *Leading American Inventors.* Freeport, N.Y.: Books for Libraries Press, 1968.

Mirksy, Jeannette, and Allan Nevins. *The World of Eli Whitney.* New York: Macmillan, 1952.

Olmsted, Denison. *Memoir of Eli Whitney, Esq.* New York: Arno Press, 1972.

# INDEX